# Editorial

'We no longer need the Norton anthologies,' a lecturer friend remarked to me recently. 'My generation [he is forty-nine] may be the last to have been brought up on the great print anthologies.' My generation (I am seventy-five) was reared on Louis Untermeyer, on Cleanth Brooks and Robert Penn Warren, and on the handsome blue hardback Oxford anthologies with their distinctive gold blocking. They soon shed their dust jackets and took up their regimental postures on the main bookshelf, where they remain and are frequently consulted.

I find it hard to imagine a life in poetry not rooted in some way in the big anthologies – chronologically ordered, perhaps, in thrall to some notion of canon, and of course designed to be rebelled against when the time is right. The time is only right when a wide range of poems has been taken to heart, connected, disconnected. And the canonical anthology shelf is not finite: new anthologies arrive and enrich it, in particular those predicated on recovering and establishing previously un- or under-regarded writing, books like Kayo Chingonyi's 2022 *More Fiya: A New Collection of Black British Poetry* or *The Penguin Book of Indian Poets* which extend the canon. There is a separate shelf for other forms of anthology, introductory of new writers, thematic, factional...

When you and your contemporaries shared an anthology, you shared pleasure, knowledge, points of specific reference, occasions for dialogue and disagreement. As evolving theories altered our acts of reading a poem we had come to know by heart became a pretext, illuminating and illuminated by contexts we overlooked when we read it first; we valued our anthologies differently.

Salespeople for the educational anthology publishers contact poetry lecturers, my friend told me, at the beginning of a new academic year offering discount deals for bulk purchases, trying to prolong the commercial lives of books which, he says, have been decisively superseded not by a new print product but by the resources of the internet. 'You can find all the poems online,' he said. Which is true, with a few caveats: there is no guarantee of the text's accuracy, especially of layout, and students need someone to provide a contents list. When you find a text on the internet, you cannot asterisk, write in the margins, add in post-it notes. You cannot thumb the foredge and hear the book purr. And you miss authoritative annotation, introductions and bibliographies.

If you share an anthology with your contemporaries, you learn early on that poetry reading is, even at a primary level, collaborative. You take things from their readings and you contribute to them. Collaboration is basic to the art itself. A poem collaborates with previous writing and can expect attentive readers to hear that collaboration. Semantic change can enhance or impoverish it. Sometimes a poem isn't aware of its connections. Anachronism has a part to play – a poem can come to know much more than its poet did.

In Dryden's 'Secular Masque' Momus can sound quite like Auden. Dryden marks the turn of a millennium whose start was marked by his death:

All, all, of a piece throughout;
Thy chase had a beast in view;
Thy wars brought nothing about;
Thy lovers were all untrue.
'Tis well an old age is out,
And time to begin a new.

Graham Greene wrests this stanza from its context and presents it as a stand-alone lyric. In Dryden Momus addresses each line to a separate 'reader' – the second to Diana, the third to Mars, the fourth to Aphrodite. Janus speaks the fifth and sixth. Dryden then draws all six lines together for the Chorus to recite. Greene is interested in the chorus, not what precedes it. The language remains Dryden's, but the extracted poem does not. Such writing thrives in an anthology and the wider contexts and collaborations it proposes.

Is it the case, as one of our younger readers put it recently, that poetry is at last outgrowing those notions of collaboration which continue to respect a canon or modernisms and their ideologically tainted legacies? Originality of another sort is possible, is it not; is indeed what creativity should nowadays be about?

These arguments bring Jack Kerouac to mind. The centenary of his birth has not been widely celebrated so far this year, any more than Philip Larkin's or Donald Davie's have. Think what we might learn if the three were drawn together, with Larkin on the east, Kerouac on the west, and Davie like Janus facing in both directions, sounding severe, of course, but allowing himself to be swayed on the one hand by the work, on the other by the theory.

Kerouac collaborated with William Burroughs on the novel *And the Hippos Were Boiled in Their Tanks*, the title drawn from an hysterical news report of a fire at a zoo in which the unhappy hippos *were* indeed boiled in their tanks – as if rehearsing for a surreal moment in later Burroughs. Kerouac, especially in what I almost called his formative years, but he kept forming and re-forming... Kerouac imagined a writing that readers would throw away as soon as they had read it, a writing which as language laid no claim on readers, did not try to snare them in a memorable skein of words. It delivered its meaning and then memory – with a diminished role – let it go. Meaning is for him *real*, and separable from the ways it is articulated, from its style. If too deeply invested in style, meaning becomes restricting, partial – political. Just as an anthology can do.

Yet I revert gratefully to the 'Letter to the Teacher' in the 1938 edition of Brooks and Warren's *Understanding Poetry*: 'This book has been conceived on the assumption that if poetry is worth teaching at all it is worth teaching as poetry. The temptation to make a substitute for the poem as the object of study is usually overpowering.' The editors rethought and adjusted their anthology, adding critical material, instructions to teacher and reader, in the 1950 edition. Kerouac at school may have been nursed, and perhaps even weaned, on the book. As reader and editor I am still – though ironically – in its thrall, and that of the other anthologies which have opened poetry out for me. I have committed several anthologies myself, less as a gate keeper than a gate maker.

# Letter to the Editor

*Rupert Loydell writes:* I was pleased to read Alan Munton's review of Steve Spence's books in PNR 265, but must insist that the poet and author is very much present in his work: Spence is the selector, editor, arranger, reviser and creator of what he has written. As an academic researcher in Modernism, Munton knows full well that collage and re-presentation have a well-established history within poetry, as does the idea of the reader assembling meaning for herself.

The rise of the digital and emerging theories of remixology have provided other ways to understand the use of what Munton calls 'quotations removed from their context', although I would argue that Spence provides a new context. No language is or can be original, and Spence (along with many other contemporary poets) has simply followed a creative course and writing process that accepts and engages with this.

*Alan Munton replies:* I really must look again at Milton and Wordsworth, and that radical Shelley, to see how they wrote like Steve Spence. And perhaps Chaucer was doing that back in the fourteenth century? Oh, you mean T.S. Eliot! But there's no going beyond him. And what a surprise to read that the author of a poem actually arranges the words themselves. This is an idea that Rupert Loydell should develop in his magazine *Stride*, where he has been publishing Spence's poems and reviews for years, and recently wrote an ecstatic review of one of the books I discussed. Though I do agree: we must think in Loydell's terms, or not at all. I was trying to show how what he dubs 'remixology' actually works, and the reader's creative part in that; evidently I've gone too far. And I was certainly interested to learn that 'no language is or can be original', and that we must all 'accept and engage' with this. Passivity before what is happening to language in these disrupted times is clearly the way forward.

# News and Notes

**The Poet of Old Hall** · Poet, bookseller and publisher Peter Scupham died on 11 June, aged eighty-nine. He was at home in Norfolk. His partner Margaret Stewart said he went, 'very quietly, with the sunshine pouring through the open French windows'. He'd received, just in time, finished copies of his last book, *Invitation to View*, and was pleased to hold it and hear what it had to say.

Peter was a contributor to the first issue of *Poetry Nation* – the second poet, after Charles Tomlinson, in that historic number – and appeared a total of seventy-five times in the next fifty years. His last contribution was to *PNR* 260, last year. *PNR* celebrated his work as a poet and eccentric Englishman on his eighty-fifth birthday in 2018 with a Scupham supplement

Michael Schmidt, his long-time editor, said: 'Peter is a poet I loved almost from my arrival in the UK. He was a superlative second-hand bookseller whose Mermaid Books catalogues were harmonies of erudition and hilarity and whose prices were always within range. His envelopes he often decorated with drawings that added to the merriment of his correspondence. The garden of the Old Hall that he and Margaret Stewart restored was a gathering-place for poets, with summer Shakespeare performances and a permanent welcome.'

He was published first by Peterloo Poets, Harry Chambers's Manchester venture, and then by OUP. Carcanet took over the OUP poetry list and he became formally Carcanet's. He knew something about publishing himself. He and his friend John Mole were proper, inky-fingered publishers, with letterpress and hand-stitching. Their Mandeville Press produced handsome, significant pamphlets and the legendary Dragon Cards.

'Few poets in my experience are as generous, cheerful and formally accomplished as Peter,' his editor said. 'As he lay preparing for death, I asked him to record some of his new poems. He roused himself and with his usual smiling precision of voice read. Margaret recorded him on her phone and this happy effort will soon be shared, along with a fine tribute by John Mole.'

In a blog, he wrote: 'When Margaret and I bought a semi-derelict and ramshackle Tudor house perched in long grass on the edge of nowhere, we eventually opened it under a scheme called "Invitation to View". The house and its putting together is one of the themes in this collection, but the invitation is seen as made by our ghosts, when what we have done and made is just one more arrangement of tantalising dust and wilderness. That invitation set apart, I would not want this book to be about studying one's X-ray plates in a deck chair, or making cumbrous farewells. I hope there is a spring lyricism, albeit tempered by a certain wintery nip.'

**Masters, believers and doubters** · The shortlists for the 2022 Forward Prizes for Poetry were announced in mid-June. The Forwards turn thirty this year and are moving house, leaving London and bravely descending on the provinces. Indeed, the prize-giving will be celebrated a couple of miles from the *PN Review* offices at Manchester University's Contact Theatre.

As usual, the shortlists – chosen this year by novelist Fatima Bhutto (chair), and poets Stephen Sexton, Rishi Dastidar, alice hiller, and Nadine Aisha Jassat – are for Best Collection (£10,000), Best First Collection (Felix Dennis Prize, £5,000) and Best Single Poem (£1,000). Chatto & Windus provides three of the shortlisted titles. The Best Collection shortlist includes:

Kaveh Akbar – *Pilgrim Bell* (Chatto)
Anthony Joseph – *Sonnets for Albert* (Bloomsbury)
Shane McCrae – *Cain Named the Animal* (Little Brown)
Kim Moore – *All the Men I Never Married* (Seren)
Helen Mort – *The Illustrated Woman* (Chatto)

The Best First Collection shortlist introduces:

Mohammed El-Kurd – *Rifqa* (Haymarket)

Holly Hopkins – *English Summer* (Penned in the Margins)

Padraig Regan – *Some Integrity* (Carcanet)

Warsan Shire – *Bless the Daughter Raised by a Voice in Her Head* (Chatto)

Stephanie Sy-Quia – *Amnion* (Granta)

The Forward Prize for Best Single Poem includes *PN Review*'s own Carl Phillips:

Louisa Campbell, 'Dog on a British Airways Airbus' (*Perverse*)

Cecilia Knapp, 'I'm Shouting I LOVED YOUR DAD at my Brother's Cat' (*Perverse*)

Nick Laird, 'Up Late' (*Granta*)

Carl Phillips, 'Scattered Snows, to the North' (*PNR*)

Clare Pollard, 'Pollen' (*Bad Lilies*)

Fatima Bhutto said: 'As the Chair of the Forward Prize judges, to spend the better part of a year thinking about poetry has been an incredible gift. The collections we pored over reminded me of the care and power strangers exert over each other in so many delicate and fragile ways. We have assembled here a collection of debut writers, masters, believers and doubters, all of them innate observers of our intimate lives.' The winners of this year's prizes will be announced on 28 November at a live event at Contact Theatre, Manchester. Lucy Macnab, Co-Executive Director of the Forward Arts Foundation, said: 'we view this partnership with Keisha Thompson and Contact as a significant step toward our future strategic vision: to move away from the dominance of London in the UK's creative and cultural life; a drive toward working more inclusively with young people, emerging voices, and diverse audiences, putting them at the centre of our practice; and working with partners that put poetry at the heart of their creative offer.' Thompson, the first practicing poet to lead a theatre as Artistic Director, said: 'Poetry has always been a big part of what we do at Contact and it's going to be so important to me as I lead the theatre. Partnering with the Forward Prizes is a wonderful way to start.'

**Wild Shetland** · The 2021 Highland Book Prize was awarded to Jen Hadfield for her collection *The Stone Age* (Picador). The prize was announced at a ceremony hosted by the Highland Society of London at Moniack Mhor, with live and online audiences.

'The poems in *The Stone Age* evoke the wild landscape of Shetland, where Hadfield lives. A member of the volunteer reading panel said, 'This exploration of neurodiversity in poetry is authentic and original. The individual poems each have a jewel-like quality that grab the reader with a host of fresh images and aperçus.'

**Griffin** · This year's Griffin Prizes have gone to Tolu Oloruntoba (Canadian winner, $65,000) for *The Junta of Happenstance* (Anstruther Books/Palimpsest Press), 'an exploration of disease, both medical and emotional' which also 'explores family dynamics, social injustice, the immigrant experience, economic anxiety and the nature of suffering'; and to the American Douglas Kearney (International winner, $65,000) for *Sho* (Wave Books) in which his 'genius, vulnerability, and virtuosity are on full display'. The judges were Adam Dickinson (Canada), Valzhyna Mort (Belarus/US), and Claudia Rankine (Jamaica/US). There were 639 entries, including 57 translations from 24 languages, submitted by 236 publishers from 16 countries.

**C. Day-Lewis** · May 22nd marked the fiftieth anniversary of the death of quondam poet laureate C. Day-Lewis, and to mark the event Wadham College, Oxford staged a one-day exhibition. From July to September the Bodleian Library are hosting a display from their Day-Lewis archive. In addition, Professor Albert Gelpi made a perceptive selection of Day-Lewis's poetry which can be viewed on the website of *Agenda*.

*O Caledonia* · Elspeth Barker, an unconventional Scot who refined her unusual existence into *O Caledonia*, published in 1991, died in April. *O Caledonia* is rooted in Barker's own eccentric life, though it begins in the wake of her imagined demise. Her Gothic settings, love of jackdaws and wild things as favoured companions, of books, and her avoidance of the boys that troubled her childhood, are vividly evoked. The natural description is brilliant and shockingly memorable.

*O Caledonia* was successful in Great Britain and in translation across Europe. By the time it was published the author was fifty-one, her partner being the poet George Barker whom she joined at the age of twenty-two (he was fifty) and finally married. She was eighty-two years old at the time of her death and her daughter the novelist Raphaela Barker said that she had died simply of old age, a plausible explanation. The story of her life would be a wonderful project for a patient nature- or life-writer. It would entail the lives of other writers, her children and step-children, and her predecessors in George Barker's affections, notably Elizabeth Smart, who seems to have engineered her romance with Mr Barker to set herself free of him.

The poet Hilary Davies, widow of Sebastian Barker and step-daughter-in-law of Elspeth, wrote to us with the sad news that Elspeth Barker's brilliant step-son Christopher, author (as photographer and designer) of *Portraits of Poets* (Carcanet/Folio Society, 1986), died four days later. Hilary remarked, 'They were links to another world, the 1940s poets, that have gone.'

**Dollies** · The great Portuguese painter Paula Rego, born in 1935, died on 8 June. She was a lover of poetry and a longstanding friend of *PN Review*, contributing cover images and ekphrastic occasions to many poets. Her principal male model and companion Anthony Rudolf is also a long-term contributor to the magazine and in *PNR* 267 we will include his poem 'Paula Rego's Studio and her "Dollies"'.

We invited her friend the poet Dan Burt to recall her as a painter and a lover of music.

# Reports

## At the Opera, and Elsewhere, with Paula Rego

### DAN BURT

*Gilda: Mio Padre!*
*Rigoletto: A te d'appresso trova*
*sol gioia il core oppresso.*
*Gilda: Oh, Quanto amore, padre mio!*

[My father!
Only with you does my heavy heart find joy.
Oh, my loving father!]

Gilda's first words, Rigoletto's reply, when she comes on stage for the first time and rushes into his arms. The octogenarian in the red plush seat beside me, Paula Rego, leans forward, intent. Her father Rigoletto exits, and Gilda begins her famous first solo aria, *Gaultier Maldè*, a paean to love for a seducer:

*GILDA (sola)*
*Gualtier Maldû...nome di lui sž amato,*
*ti scolpisci nel core innamorato!*
*Caro nome che il mio cor*
*festi primo palpitar*
*[le] dell'amor delizie*
*mi dši sempre rammentar!*

[Gilda (alone)
Walter Maldû`name of the man I love
be thou engraved upon my lovesick heart!
Beloved name, the first to move
the pulse of love within my heart
thou shalt remind me ever
of the delights of love!]

Paula is rapt, and remains so until the curtain falls on Rigoletto's howl of pain, his dead daughter's half sacked body cradled in his arms. Paula dabs tears meandering down her face before the principals take their bows.

That performance several years ago was the last of perhaps three *Rigolettos* over fifteen years Paula and I watched together at the ROH, she as my guest, before creeping frailty as she aged cost me an opera-date. Each curtain-fall found her the same, a transported, tearful painter marrow deep in a tragedy she understood in her bones.

Twenty years before, I'd been taken to her Camden Town studio for the first time. Scattered across several large ground-floor, high ceilinged, concrete-floored rooms were dolls and dummies from small to huge, heaped or in isolation, with human, animal, hybrid or fantasy features, some store bought, some her son-in-law Ron Mueck made. All in time materialized in her works. Paintings and drawings from sketches to finished sat on easels or on the floor against the walls. An assistant who doubled as her customary female model busied herself on the left side of the room, next to a boom-box playing Rigoletto. Surrounded by this surreal crowd, accompanied by Verdi, an animated, elfin septuagenarian in a green sweater waited to show me round.

Later visits revealed different dummies, props, and equipment: a life size, fissured-face woman in black that Paula called *Aunty Death*, a huge, brown, formless *Pillow Man*, infant dolls used in Rego's Foundling Hospital series; a small lift that allowed her to paint large works, like the eight-foot-tall *Wedding of the Last King of Portugal*. New paintings and drawings in process or completed populated each visit.

The one constant was music from the boom box, if not bel canto, then Amalia Rodriguez, fado singer and Portuguese national icon, wailing of *Coimbra*, of Inêz de Castille, dead loves, distant homelands.

Rego's work was not new to me when I entered her studio, nor were the *School of London* figurative painters – Andrews, Auerbach, Bacon, Freud, Kitaj – among whom she's numbered[1]. Her triptych *Martha, Mary and Magde-*

---

1 Five of the six School of London painters were, like Rego, emigrés in Britain: Auerbach (Germany), Bacon (Ireland), Freud (Austria), Kitaj (USA), Rego (Portugal). Perhaps this helps explain the source of the alienation redolent in their art.

lene, *Retouched* (*Martha*)², which her Marlborough Gallery dealers dubbed *The Saints*, had been a favourite of mine since I first saw it hanging in their Albemarle street gallery in 1999, the year it was painted, and several years before I met Paula. In some of her works the face and form of Tony Rudolph, a literary acquaintance, and Rego's long-time companion, model, and escort on our opera evenings fostered an illusion of familiarity with work I was viewing for the first time.

What was a revelation on entering her studio was Paula's passion for bel canto and fado. Asked how she came to be listening to *Rigoletto*, she replied she always worked with music playing, mostly bel canto and fado, that *Rigoletto* was her grail, and Amalia Rodriguez her *fadista* of choice. Hearing they were mine as well, she beamed. I promised to invite her to *Rigoletto* as my guest when the ROH next staged it.

Down the years after that visit, at the opera, dinner parties at my flat, book launches, openings, dinner in her honour at the Tate, our talk touched on art, poetry, and Portuguese novels; on tyrants, Fascism, the Church, predatory priests, affairs and marriages; on her dead husband Victor Willing, whom she thought her works' best critic; on abortion, cruelty to and infanticide of bastards; on rape and war and misery. But things she said to me are not what come to mind when I try to understand the mainsprings of her work. What do, other than her art itself, are three nouns prompted by writing *Martha*, observing *Rigoletto* ensorcell Paula at the ROH, and witnessing her friendship with a Madeiran housekeeper: autobiography, intensity, and *saudade*.

Before Tony Rudolph asked me to contribute to an homage volume for Rego's eightieth birthday, I had thought neither hard nor long about the beating heart of her art. Writing *Martha* I came to see the triptych as a comprehensive autobiography of a painter in three panels, a work unlike any other in art history, though that's not my field. Appropriating Catholic hagiography to comment on and subtly intensify her life that led me to judge her own history composed the essence of her oeuvre.

*Rigoletto* was a home movie for Paula. Watching it she

2 See images accompanying *Martha* [below].

metamorphosed into Gilda; the Duke of Mantua became Victor Willing; Rigoletto her father. She identified so intensely and completely with the tragedy unfolding behind the orchestra she seemed to vanish into the performance. Observing her at *Rigolettos* fostered my belief that the same capacity for passionately reliving seminal events in her life was the source of her art's scalding energy and subject matter, its colours, forms, and fantasies.

There is no single, simple English word for the Portuguese noun *saudade*. Perhaps the closest English approximation is a deep melancholy sprung from longing for a lost love or homeland. *Saudade* is the essence of fado – its lyrics teem with the word.

Conceicao Moreira, a Madeiran, had been my invaluable and much-loved housekeeper for more than fifteen years when Paula Rego first came to my flat for dinner. An emigré like Rego, she had been long in England, her English good, her taxes paid, but most of her family and all her heart still dwelled in the hills outside Funchal. For Madeira and Portuguese culture Conceicao felt *saudade*.

The Portuguese esteem Paula as a national treasure. The expectation that she might materialize at my dinner table was for Conceicao akin to anticipating a visit from the Virgin. Paula arrived, Conceicao was introduced to her, and they fell into a spirited conversation in Portuguese which Paula reluctantly ended when we were called to dinner.

A friendship blossomed. They talked together in Portuguese for 10-15 minutes whenever Paula came to my flat. She invited Conceicao to her studio for tea. One Christmas, Paula gave Conceicao two drawings she made based on Conceicao's anecdotes about her granddaughter. Properly framed, they hang in Conceicao's house, the only treasure she has to bequeath to her granddaughter.

From observing Paula and Conceicao together, I believe their friendship was in part rooted in Paula's *saudade* for the Portuguese land, sea and peasantry of her childhood, and that the same melancholic longing infuses her art.

Paula Rego longs for her vanished world no more; she died on 8 June 2022.

# Martha, Mary and Magdalene Retouched

## DAN BURT

*for Paula*

In the left panel, Martha sits,
thighs akimbo on a tall stool,
pastels open by bare right foot,
eyes raised, brush poised to put
on canvas cruelty, fear, rape;
not Rossetti's ethereal amateur,
but novice worthy of the ur-sister
who told off Christ, and maybe,
set him to washing-up after tea.

A woman cradles a man
in the centre painting, a Pietà
unlike Michelangelo's five centuries ago
in cream Carrara; no Mary bowed,
bearing her son on Golgotha
but frowning, ramrod, tempered lady,
on her knees a tall, thin, pasty body
in boxer shorts, a male too old
to be her child, her look too cold
to be a mother's, more like the stare
of the jilted lover
watching Aeneas bear away into the north.

The story ends with image pulled
from cinquecento Dutch devotional,
*The Magdalen Reading* –
lime robe neck to toes,
white head scarf, bible,
cabinet against her back –
changed to pleated, knee-length skirt,
unzipped Barbour, plum beret,
battered, ransacked, Churchill case
bracing the reader's carapace,
thick-soled, black calf-length boots;
a seated gypsy in a *conte moral* –
life shrunk to clothes on your back,
a bare room, a paperback.

Three modern saints
for an atheist's wall,
pastels on paper on aluminium,
feminize the Gospels
with the painter's autobiography.

# Sounding a Way

## Charles Causley's 'Angel Hill'

### VAHNI CAPILDEO

Although the sea was not close by (in Cornish terms), in Launceston, the fortified border town on the river Tamar, staying in Cyprus Well, the late poet Charles Causley's cottage, I felt as if the sea must be close by. Turning sharp left out beneath the thirteenth-century Southgate Arch, and looking longingly but not too lingeringly at the film posters and cakes of the nearby cafés, you cross over Dockacre Road and begin a steep descent. Angel Hill, Ridgegrove Hill: the slope reminds me of the narrow ways cut into Trinidad's Northern Range, which I know mostly by car, seeing other cars squeeze past on hairpin bends, and the Atlantic gleam greatly in occasional rifts in the sharply shelving, forested red rock. The sense of peril and acceleration was the same; of humans perched twiggily on geological movements; of four-dimensional maps that squeezed like accordions to play bittersweet histories.

Within Cyprus Well, the cottage, there are different ways of sounding the space. You could orientate yourself by the inexplicable rustle in early evening from Charles Causley's room, as if someone were shuffling papers or moving about at the window. Upstairs, you could sink into birdsong, in spring. Going downstairs, you could wake up the grandfather clock as you brushed past it, at the foot of the modest central staircase. The insides would tick-knock, as if asking to be set going. So, you wind the clock, and add chimes to the bells that already ring from churches on all sides. As if underwater, you are in a sounding-space. Perhaps the buried pre-medieval well still adds its quality of depth and liquidity to the building's interior.

It seemed natural – sitting in the study where Charles Causley played the piano, and where (it seems from the red-pencilled dynamics on popular sheet music) people sang – to read aloud. Reading aloud, not as a performance, but as a form of sounding. At Southwark, the Anglican Franciscans had introduced me to *lectio divina*, a monastic practice of shared, slow reading-aloud, with imaginative contemplation. I had never heard anything like the friendly silence shared at length between each line. I adapted this technique for a shared reading and reflection session in Trinidad, outdoors on the Savannah, beneath the trees, filmed just as we were locking down. It seemed obvious to me that shared, slow sounding took you to other places than 'practical criticism', the quick pulling-apart of text. Acknowledged or unacknowledged, *lectio divina* is, or can be, a source, or current, for conemporary poetry and understanding. Steve Ely, in *Lectio Violant* (Shearsman, 2021), applies this technique of attention to Biblical passages to create secular poems inspired by them, drenched with the voluptuous, complex violence of our ever-hotter environment. It is an extraordinary book.

Here I shall offer a 'slow reading' of Charles Causley's enigmatic poem, 'Angel Hill', adapting this tradition of attention. 'Angel Hill', an eight-stanza ballad, shows a flashing-eyed sailor turning up at the door of the poem's speaker. The sailor claims heart-kinship. The speaker rejects him repeatedly, with the refrain, *'No, never'*. Is the sailor an angel (the angel of death?), or Christ (embodiment of perfect love), coming knocking? Is this a love that dare not speak its name, sweetness at sea bitterly bricked up by respectability on land? Does it matter? What mattered to me was Causley's flexuous use of a traditional form, running line-shapes backwards and forwards, to bring the strange visitor more and more brightly and sadly before us, while the rejection sounds more hollow with every repetition.

What will happen during a slow reading-aloud? I encourage you to try the following technique for yourself. The joy of sharing slow reading in a group, of course, is that aspects of the poem flash up for, or stick with, people, most unexpectedly, forming a communal response, like an ancient mosaic on the floor of a natural pool, where we're sitting with our feet in the water, the light bending on our limbs as we piece together pictures.

On the first reading aloud, listen for a word or phrase that catches your attention. Listen simply. What really catches your attention? You're not listening for a key word, or the right phrase. What stands out, to you? For me, the word 'bound' stood out as never before, though I know this poem well, have heard it read aloud by others, and in the song setting by Jim Causley. The sailor is reminding the cottage-dweller of the bread and brine they tasted together 'As I bound your wounds and you

bound mine'. The abrupt rhythms of life at sea, described by the sailor, who comes walking with his bundle, contrast with the steady life of the man who has grown 'too proud'. I hear 'bound' as refusing to rhyme with 'wound' (injury) but rhyming with the word that isn't there, 'wound' as in shroud, or entwining lovers, or the metal of a ring of a pledge. I feel 'bound' as the bounding main, the sea of sea chanteys. I see 'bound' as echoing the word-shape of 'proud'. Somehow the speaker's pride is bound with pain, and the sailor arrives as a promise and memory of healing...

On the second reading aloud, find something that catches your attention for what seems to be a symbolic, or deeper, meaning. Be honest. You may pick up on something marginal or fractional, and yet arc out into a wider light. What struck me was the entirety of the penultimate stanza:

His eye it flashed like a lightning-dart
And still as stone then stood my heart.
My heart as a granite stone was still
And he said, 'My friend, but I think you will.'
*No, never,* said I.

Wouldn't lightning crack stone? Instead, the heart stops, like the grandfather clock's pendulum in Cyprus Well cottage. Yet, in contradiction to what seems to be happening in the poem, let's not forget the locality of Causley's poems. Let's visit nearby St Mary Magdalene church. If you walk up Angel Hill and turn right onto Dockacre Road, you can cut up some steps that will lead you to a green terrace, then the churchyard, then the back of this extraordinary building, where the granite blocks are carved with such delicacy that they look like jacquard, damask, lace: some type of ceremonial or wedding fabric. Perhaps a transformation is beginning in the obdurate *No, never,* speaker, after all...

On the third reading aloud, think of something you would ask or say, if you could enter the poem's world. I have to confess that sometimes, in *lectio divina*, I 'ask' someone who is not explicitly named in the text but can be supposed to be present: an animal, a bystander, an innkeeper...an angel. Here I want to ask them whether they both remember that together they 'whistled to moon and sun'; do their memories match up? What were they feeling, when they whistled? Was it a carefree moment, or a moment of profound, unspoken connexion? What were they whistling? Was it tuneless, happy whistling, like my mother's father used to do at home as he went about practical tasks of carpentry or tailoring or childcare? Were they good at whistling, doing a duet of some tune they both loved? That moment of being on the deep, looking up at the sky, and tuning their breath together: I want to ask them to re-sound that...

On the fourth reading aloud, what application of the poem can you make to your own life? I leave you there and hope that you will go to find it.

# Letter from Wales

## SAM ADAMS

John Davies's *A History of Wales* tells how this land was incorporated into England by statute in 1536, and gained thereby the right to representation in the English parliament. With a population of rather more than a quarter of a million, it had twenty-six MPs. The famous, or infamous, Act of Union also proscribed the use of the Welsh language by those in public office. This meant that the Welsh gentry, who retained a pivotal role in administrative and cultural affairs, had perforce to become fluent in English. Thus began the slow decay, from the head, of the daily habit of Welsh. Even so, the proportion of the population who were Welsh speaking continued high deep into the nineteenth century – as much as two-thirds according to Davies. It is arguable Wales might well have remained a predominantly Welsh-speaking rural backwater, with convenient resorts offering modest mountain peaks and attractive coastal scenery to the English on vacation, when the continent was cut off due to fog in the channel or some other local difficulty. Prior to the invention of the steam-engine, the only sources of power were wind, water and the physical strength of man and beast, all in some measure unreliable. Coal and iron, metal-founding and steam-driven transport were the basis of industrial development, and Wales, blessed (or cursed?) with exploitable deposits of coal and ore, had a major role in the revolution. Heavy industry, particularly in the extensive South Wales coalfield, brought an influx of English speakers over the Bristol Channel – that is, mostly from Somerset, Gloucestershire and Cornwall, as threads of ancestry in my own family and thousands of others testify. Surges of native Welsh speakers from the west and north, similarly attracted by the promise (often broken) of decently paid and regular work, for a time maintained a semblance of linguistic balance in the south, and there was a temporary burgeoning of Welsh culture hereabouts, but by the end of the nineteenth century the decline had set in and seemed irreversible: at the 1901 Census, 34.8 percent of the population of Wales declared they were Welsh speakers; in 2011 that relative amount had fallen to 19 percent.

So much for the familiar old story, which I have certainly outlined before. However, there are promising signs that an increase will be registered with the results of the 2021 Census, largely due to popular demand for and increased provision of Welsh-medium education in the past decade. Now the government in Cardiff has announced its official aim to boost the number of Welsh speakers to one million by 2050. This will entail doubling the number of teachers able to teach through the medium of Welsh throughout the school system from about two and a half to five thousand within a generation. The Senedd, where business is conducted bi-lingually, has recently published a research document indicating the direction of development of the policy. There has already been substantial enlargement of provision in schools, but it looks to grow the number of Welsh-medium playgroups (*Cylchoedd Meithrin*), and the numbers of children progressing from the playgroups into Welsh-medium primary and thence to secondary education. All this will, in turn, have implications for post-school education, including expansion in the Welsh universities sector, where currently five hundred courses (including, for example, law, history, business and physics) can be pursued through the medium of Welsh. And there are fresh initiatives to improve provision in the hitherto neglected further education sector. The government acknowledges that all the aspiration and planning, all the required investment, will not ultimately have the desired effect unless the language is used by people in their daily lives. Some 10 percent of the population currently speak Welsh daily; it anticipates an increase to 20 percent by 2050.

I have been reading *The Bilingual Brain* (Allen Lane) by the late Albert Costa (1970–2017). The book makes us think again about how children acquire language from the sounds of speech without the gaps that distinguish individual words on the printed page, and about the differing degrees of bilingual competence achieved by individuals from near perfect command of both languages to far more common disparity in proficiency between them. Costa's research demonstrates that, at four months, babies are able to differentiate between two languages as similar as Spanish and Catalan. Yet more wonderful, between four and six months old, if they have been exposed to French and English, they are able to differentiate between those languages by watching videos of people speaking them 'without sound'! Who knew babies were such close observers of a speaker's lips? Does bilingualism have a downside? Costa notes the monolingual tends to have a wider vocabulary – marginally – in his sole means of communication than the bilingual in his 'first' language, but much depends on whether individuals spend more time playing football or reading; or as readers, whether their time is spent with the *Daily Mail* or Shakespeare.

Back in the 1960s/70s, I turned my nose up at early manifestations of experimental, concrete and performance poetry, which was most vibrantly represented here by Peter Finch. A youthful veteran of the 'Poetry Wars', in the course of which he was offered and declined the opportunity to edit *The Poetry Review*, Peter brushed off my demur and carried on writing and performing – for which we are all grateful. He started publishing poems as a teenager and, at nineteen in 1966, launched a mimeographed magazine, *Second Aeon,* from his home in Cardiff. The following year he gave his first public reading. By 1968, already linked with Bob Cobbing, Jeff Nuttal and other experimental poets, he launched 'No Walls Readings' at a circuit of local pubs. His successful melding of creativity and literary entrepreneurship was noted: he became, successively, manager of 'Oriel', the Welsh Arts Council's bookshop in Cardiff (1973–98), where he created a flourishing institution which hosted readings and housed one of best collections of published poetry in the UK, then (1998–2011) chief executive of *Yr Academi Gymreig*/the Welsh Academy of Writers, which had sunk into intermittent low-level activity, and turned it into a functioning literature promotion agency. His energy and commitment to literature as business did not sprag his personal creative flair and industry as a writer and performer in the UK, USA and various European countries. There are not many who have given readings in places as diverse as Nice, Omaha, Hay, St Petersburg, Aberaeron, Ilkley and Baku. Cardiff remains his HQ, however, and in 2002, with the publication of *Real Cardiff,* the first of four volumes on the city, he stepped out as psychogeographer, a calling that has taken him around the coast of South Wales (*Edging the Estuary*, 2013), and to the USA and back (*The Roots of Rock*, 2015).

Peter Finch was seventy-five earlier this year. Seren celebrated the occasion with a two-volume *Collected Poems*, volume I 1968–1997, and II 1997–2021. Together they run to just shy of a thousand pages. The launch, in Cardiff of course, attracted a big audience. Wherever he appears he earns applause, and laughter in the right places, for a personable and polished performance that combines sharp wit and carefully rehearsed riffing on words and meanings with sobering reflections on the human condition. It would not be a surprise to learn a lot of books were sold.

# Selbstgefühl

## ALBERTO MANGUEL

The woman who taught me my first languages (English and German) was not my mother but a refugee from Germany who had been engaged by my parents as my governess when I was only a few months old. Her name was Ellin Slonitz and she had escaped Nazi Germany with her parents, her sister and her brother, shortly after the Old Synagogue of Stuttgart had been set on fire during Kristallnacht. Her father was a Czech engineer who had migrated to Germany during World War I. Ellin was born on 22 November 1914 in Rotenburg an der Fulda, Hessen. She died in Florida on 8 March 1995, four months after her eightieth birthday.

I was born in Buenos Aires, but since my father had been appointed ambassador to Israel, when I was still a baby we moved to Tel-Aviv, to a recently built house on Trumpeldor Straße. Ellin and I were allotted the basement: a large room whose windows were four small rectangles close to the ceiling through which I could see the grass of the square garden outside and a strip of sky. The four palm trees that stood in the middle of the lawn were invisible from my windows, and I always felt surprised at their appearance when Ellin took me out into the garden to play, as if I expected them to vanish while I was sleeping. Their daily rediscovered presence was very reassuring.

Once (I must have been four or five), while I was building a landscape for my lead-metal toys (I had a magnificent collection of both farm and wild animals), I told Ellin, who as usual sat at her table working at her electric knitting machine, that our room was too big for only the two of us. Our basement contained both our beds, three tables, several straight-backed and uncomfortable chairs, one plump armchair, and a colossal wooden wardrobe with looking-glass doors that duplicated the length of the room.

'*Ein Werdender wird immer dankbar sein*,' Ellin quoted. 'If you're hopeful, you'll always be grateful.' And she went on to tell me that in Stuttgart, she and her family were locked in their too-small apartment for months because her father thought it was too dangerous for them, as Jews, to go out into the street, but that in spite of that, they lived in hope that one day things would change. Ellin's brother had managed to escape to England to join the resistance and his room was occupied at once by a young German soldier whom they were constrained to lodge. Ellin remembered (she was barely an adolescent at the time) the young man coming back to their apartment every night and tearing of his Nazi uniform, and trampling on it, cursing and weeping. I didn't ask her why, but I hoped that we wouldn't have to share our basement with anyone else, whether a soldier or not.

Ellin would have me learn by heart long poems by Gustav Schwab, Goethe and Heine: *Erlkönig, Die Granadiere, Der Reiter und der Bodensee, Das Gewitter*. If I said that I was tired of memorizing poems, she would always answer: '*Des Teufels liebstes Möbelstück ist die lange Bank*', ['The Devil's best-beloved piece of furniture is a bench to lie on']. And she'd tell me how useful she had found the poems she had been instructed to learn by heart as a child when, in her adolescence, she was forced to spend a year in an iron lung during a polio outbreak. She would remain motionless inside the contraption, like in a coffin, reciting to herself the poems she knew to hasten the hours. The device was developed in 1928 in the United States, so hers must have been one of the first to be used in Germany.

Her accounts of her confinements – first obliged to lie inside the iron cocoon because of her polio, then forced to stay in her apartment because of the Nazi threat – made me think of a couple of the fairy tales I loved, Snow White in her glass box and Rapunzel trapped in her tower. Since my earliest childhood reality translated itself for me into stories, and it was in stories that I learned about the world. Normally the historical and political events through which we live daily appear to us in fragments – a snippet of news, the opinion of a neighbour, an overheard comment – and only later, much later, do these fragments coalesce into a historical narration. For me the narration came first, the story with its beginning, middle and end, and only later did I identify the vicissitudes of the protagonist or the ins and outs of the plot with events in my own life. Because I knew nothing of the crippling disease nor, to my later shame, of the Nazis, I imagined Ellin's first confinement as a coffin like the one the dwarfs had set up for the sleeping princess, the second as a prison imposed by a wicked witch. In a vague way, I compared my basement to the magical tower and judged that I could endure Rapunzel's confinement if I had my things with me, my toys and my books. But I didn't think I could bear being trapped in Snow White's coffin, however convinced I might be of the arrival of the rescuing prince, if the ceiling of my basement were lowered down to my nose as I lay face up on my bed.

My childhood basement was not, of course, comparable with any of those other confinements. I wasn't trapped in an iron box: I could move about as I wanted and I could sleep in a comfortable bed; soldiers weren't waiting outside the door to march me to a place from which there was no return. I was taken outside often: to the beach, to the park, to foreign cities. Much later, as an adult, long after I had entered the social fold and learned the conventions of social interaction, my early sense of confinement came back to me in a rush of nostalgia. Or not confinement, but isolation rather, a sense of being in a place in which it was not necessary to learn the manners and codes of others, a sense that there was no one else there, just as before there was no one except Ellin and my books.

In a forced confinement like that of prison or a hiding-place or a hospital room, conventions and niceties have to be relearned. Common rights and freedoms, such as freedom of speech and of movement, are curtailed or entirely suppressed. A hospital has this in common with a prison (I've been in both): you surrender your body to others and submit to others' handling, you have to ask permission to leave your cell or room, you have to mind your words because not everything can be said, and then not to everyone. The inhabitants of Mann's Magic Mountain and Kafka in his tubercular ward, Boethius and the Count of Montecristo in their cells, Anne Frank and Miss Havisham in their seclusions, experience these restrictions for a vast variety of reasons, some unjustly imposed on them (Anne Frank) some self-imposed (Miss Havisham). All have to learn new norms of behaviour and new daily routines. Their customary world has been annihilated and they have to build their own new brave ones.

But in every state of confinement, there is always someone else beyond the locked door: those who knew us and miss us, or have perhaps forgotten us; those who go about their lives unaware of our cloistered existence; those who go about their business and whom we will one day, perhaps, cross on the street and get to know or not. Their absence defines us. There is always a multitude outside – in a state of war, a political crisis, an interregnum of peace, an epidemic – that makes us, even in solitary seclusion, incarnate the contrary of aloneness. In Camus' *La Peste*, the narrator observes that, at the height of the pervading sickness, the priest, giving his sermon to a beleaguered flock, no longer speaks of 'you' but of 'we'.

When at the age of nine or ten I read *The Adventures of Robinson Crusoe*, I tried to imagine myself on a desert island, struggling to build for myself the things that Crusoe built to make his life endurable. Since I had no companions except for Ellin, I was thoroughly accustomed to occupying myself at the times when Ellin wasn't giving me a lesson or taking me on an outing. I was not made to attend school where I would have met other children my age; later, when my brothers were born, they lived with their own governess in another part of the house, and I was only taken to play with them about once a week. That was the extent of my social interaction with other children. And yet, I think I enjoyed my solitude because I never felt alone. I learned to read at a very early age, three or four, so that, when Ellin could or would not read to me, I discovered that I could journey through my books on my own. I never had to wait to see how a story developed, except if I willingly chose to prolong the excruciating suspense of not knowing what came next. I was not taught patience.

Ellin would not talk much about her early years and I didn't learn about the Nazis until well into my adolescence. My family, though Jewish on both sides, lived entirely in the present and, for me, the past was something of which I learned in history books. Ellin tutored me, among other subjects, in ancient history, and the history of Europe up to about the Napoleonic wars (she disapproved of Napoleon as a man but recognized that he was a good strategist.) Of the two World Wars she said nothing. But from time to time, a story would emerge, casually, as an illustration of a fact she wanted to teach me, or as an anecdote related to something she felt I needed to learn. I think her experiences built in her an unconscious power of resilience, a strength to survive in the most difficult circumstances. And because she wasn't aware of that strength, I did not recognize it then. For me as a child, Ellin was merely the expected presence of someone (the only one) who looked after me, cared for me, taught me, guided me with whatever lights she had acquired. She grew to love me, I think. I never quite admitted to myself that I loved her too.

Perhaps because I had a vague sense that I was missing the daily care of my natural parents, that the fleeting images of my father in his grey silk suit, and my mother in her evening gowns were not enough. Ellin told me that once, when we had gone to Paris accompanying my mother (I must have been five at the time), I crept into my mother's room, pulled out several of her expensive dresses from the closet and threw them out of the window, into the street. When Ellin scolded me for this, I felt furious at her. I didn't want to understand (or maybe I was not capable of understanding) to whom my anger was really addressed.

Only after I began high school did I start to have a sense of what we call history and its sequence of interlinked events. I learned to fit details of everyday life in what appeared to be a much vaster canvas, a mural depicting *ad infinitum* occurrence after occurrence and character after character. Again, my vocabulary came from my books, and History (capital H) seemed to me an unwieldy novel into which I dipped from time to time, landing on a certain paragraph that I happened to find interesting but with the nagging sense that I lacked the framing story. When later I was told by one of my professors about Plato's myth of the cave, I felt a kinship between my view of history and that of the cave's inhabitants: we both were watching a shadow-play, not knowing if the tale that we believed to be reading was the true one. I couldn't see the real performers, only their fleeting projections on the wall.

Ellin was not remarkably intelligent and (maybe because of this) she lacked almost entirely a sense of humour. At the age of four or five I discovered this curious dearth in her. Watching a 7-millimetre film that showed Chaplin slip on a banana peel, she would remark: 'Why did he not see the banana peel? Poor man, it must hurt terribly to fall on his back like that!' Later, as an adult, in Toronto, I went to see a Czech one-man clown show called 'The Queen and Her Fool', the single actor taking on both roles. The performance consisted of a series of sketches in which the Fool blundered at whatever he was ordered to do, and the angry Queen would punish him for his blunders. We roared with laughter. Half-way through the play, as the Fool was being beaten by the Queen, once again the actor stepped out of his role, faced the audience and said to us: 'I am being beaten. And you laugh?' I was reminded of Ellin, and I realized that what I had understood to be the lack of a sense of humour was perhaps an excess of empathy. In Tel-Aviv, her best friend, perhaps her only friend, was a wizened little German woman with a deep throaty laugh. I don't remember her name. One day I noticed a number written on the woman's arm and asked Ellin what it meant. Without explaining, Ellin simply said: 'You must never ask her about it. It is something that belongs only to her own self.' The word Ellin used was 'Selbstgefühl'.

Perhaps the relationship that confinement establishes between the presence outside and the sense of self within (the Selbstgefühl) is both one of enlightenment and of opposition. The latter is implied in Christa Wolf's notion that 'conflicts seize the whole person, force him to his knees and destroy his sense of self.' ['Die Konflikte ergreifen den ganzen Menschen, zwingen ihn in die Knie und vernichten sein Selbstgefühl'. Nachdenken über Christa T. p.110]. The former is the sense I read in Martin Buber's precept of 'zu-sich–selber-kommen', 'to arrive at oneself' to arrive at the knowledge of oneself through the knowledge of the existence of someone outside the door, whether Elijah or the wolf. 'In the ice of solitude,' Buber says in Between Man and Man (p.150) that 'man becomes most inexorably a question to himself, and just because the question pitilessly summons and draws into play his most secret life he becomes an experience to himself.' Ellin would have agreed.

Questioning oneself within the confines of one's own identity, and questioning oneself in relationship to others, are two very different skills or gifts. Confinement grants us Selbstgefühl, but not necessarily a sense of the others, except as a vague presence outside the door, an absence felt by implication. The confinements that Ellin underwent prepared her, perhaps, for later understand-

ings of who she was, in a quiet, submissive manner, never interested in exploring too far or too deep her own landscapes. But it did nothing to teach her the conventions of interaction with others. Social conflicts might not have destroyed the little she possessed of self-esteem, but it made her cower before the presence of any kind of authority: her employers (my parents), the rest of the staff at the embassy, other immigrants like herself (with very few exceptions, like her German friend). Being a German Jew, Ellin believed in Kultur, in spite of what seemed to have sprung from it in the twentieth century. She never lost faith in it, neither believing it to be ineffectual because it had not prevented the rise of Hitler, or because it had not managed to make the world a better place. She was profoundly convinced that I had to recite the dates of the Napoleonic wars in order to understand what Heine's two grenadiers were talking about; I had to know that the system of Copernicus replaced that of Ptolemy in our understanding of the skies; I had to differentiate between a mastaba and a common pyramid; I should be able to list all the capitals of Europe and all the Roman emperors. And because she believed so fervently in that need for Kultur I believed in it too, and enjoyed believing in it.

When we returned to Buenos Aires and I began my life of interaction with others beyond the confines of the basement room we had left behind, Ellin, who was now charged with looking after my sister, was forced to enter the social realm to interact with people whom she did not know, in a language that was not hers. And realizing how inadequate she was in her dealings with others, her faith in Kultur made her suppose that these skills could be learned, and she enrolled in a Dale Carnegie course (in Spanish), to learn 'How to Win Friends and Influence People'. She took me with her.

The old philosopher Protagoras, in Plato's dialogue of that name, tells Socrates a myth to explain why human beings, though they may have the skills to fashion instruments and weapons, lack the political savvy to create a just and fair society. 'Once upon a time there were gods only, and no mortal creatures,' Protagoras begins his tale. 'But when the time came that these also should be created, the gods fashioned them out of earth and fire and various mixtures of both elements in the interior of the earth; and when they were about to bring them into the light of day, they ordered Prometheus and Epimetheus to equip them, and to distribute to them severally their proper qualities. Epimetheus said to Prometheus: 'Let me distribute, and you inspect.' This was agreed, and Epimetheus made the distribution. There were some to whom he gave strength without swiftness, while he equipped the weaker with swiftness; some he armed, and others he left unarmed; and devised for the latter some other means of preservation, making some large, and having their size as a protection, and others small, whose nature was to fly in the air or burrow in the ground; this was to be their way of escape. Thus did he compensate them with the view of preventing any race from becoming extinct. And when he had provided against their destruction by one another, he contrived also a means of protecting them against the seasons of heaven; clothing them with close hair and thick skins sufficient to defend them against the winter cold and able to resist the summer heat, so that they might have a natural bed of their own when they wanted to rest; also he furnished them with hoofs and hair and hard and callous skins under their feet. Then he gave them varieties of food – herb of the soil to some, to others fruits of trees, and to others roots, and to some again he gave other animals as food. And some he made to have few young ones, while those who were their prey were very prolific; and in this manner the race was preserved. Thus did Epimetheus, who, not being very wise, forgot that he had distributed among the brute animals all the qualities which he had to give-and when he came to man, who was still unprovided, he was terribly perplexed. Now while he was in this perplexity, Prometheus came to inspect the distribution, and he found that the other animals were suitably furnished, but that man alone was naked and shoeless, and had neither bed nor arms of defence. The appointed hour was approaching when man in his turn was to go forth into the light of day; and Prometheus, not knowing how he could devise his salvation, stole the mechanical arts of Hephaestus and Athene, and fire with them (they could neither have been acquired nor used without fire), and gave them to man. Thus man had the wisdom necessary to the support of life, but political wisdom he had not; for that was in the keeping of Zeus.' In the case of Ellin, Zeus never relinquished his hold on this particular wisdom.

Ellin had arrived with her family in South America in the last months of 1947, the year before I was born. When the ship docked in Asunción (the port is now in disuse and has been transferred to another Paraguayan city), they were greeted by a display of flags bearing black swastikas. Paraguay (Ellin's father didn't know this) was the first country in South America to allow, in 1931, a political party with national-social affiliations. Later, discovering that a cousin of mine bore the name of Adolfo (in honour of my maternal grandfather), Ellin told me in passing that the Paraguayan chief of police had christened his son Adolfo Hiroito in homage to his two heroes.

A few weeks after their arrival, Ellin's father committed suicide, and her mother died shortly afterwards. Ellin only mentioned this to me once, in later years, and made no further comment. Whatever strength had grown and spread within her to sustain like a scaffolding her *Selbstgefühl* was reluctant to be made explicit. The English word 'demure' does not convey the full sense of what is meant by the German word *Sittsamkeit*, which Robert Walser, in *The Walk*, employs to speak of '*seine ihm angeborene Sittsamkeit zu unterwühlen*', 'subverting his innate demureness', but 'demureness' is the wrong word. In Ellin, it was an unspoken ethical notion, akin to gestures that must remain private like our private morning ablutions.

Ellin took on a position as governess in the house of a Jewish-German family, looking after two young girls. The first night at her employers' house she fell off the high cot that she had been allotted in the girls' bedroom, and broke an arm. Not wanting to wake her charge for fear that she might lose her job, her *Sittsamkeit* caused her to lie in what must have been terrible pain on the floor until she was discovered on the following morning. Throughout the rest of her life, her left arm remained weak and I remember seeing her massage it vigorously from time to time, during the long nights when, to distract herself from her recurrent insomnia, she would sit at her electric knitting-machine, sweeping the strand of wool back and forth with her right hand. The swoosh-swoosh of the machine lulled me to sleep as effectively as any lullaby.

Ellin's sister Renate had met an Argentinian man with an English surname, who asked her to marry him and live with him in Buenos Aires. Renate suggested that Ellin accompany them. Two years later, at the beginning of 1949, Ellin answered the ad my father had placed in the *Yidische Zaitung* nine months after I was born, looking for a nanny to look after me in Israel, where he had been appointed ambassador by Perón. The interview took place at the City Hotel (in which, years later, the Dale Carnegie course would take place). Ellin handed over to my father her passport and work permit. I seem to have been a very unpleasant baby, shrieking at the top of my voice, and Ellin felt unwilling to look after such an impossible child. My father, short of time, told her he would not return her documents unless she took on the position. Ellin was obliged to accept and we sailed off to the newly-created State of Israel. By then, Ellin's *Selbstgefühl* was not strong.

Did Ellin see her entire life consisting of stages of confinement, of transitioning from one cloistered space to another? First, the space of her body that trapped her during her adolescence inside an iron lung, and that later prevented her from free movements because of constant pain throughout her thin body: stabs in her left arm, headaches that led to insomnia, and because of what I suspect was stomach cancer, cramps in her abdomen that made her restrict her diet to a few boiled vegetables and broth. Then her confinement in the family house under threat from the Nazis, a threat that pursued her across the ocean and met her in South America when she arrived. Finally, her confinement in our basement in Tel-Aviv, from where she emerged occasionally to take me on an outing or (very rarely) alone, to meet her German friend. When she left Argentina in the late seventies, after I had wandered off to Europe and my sister had grown up and needed her no longer, she took a position as companion to an elderly Jewish-American lady in New York. She came to visit me once, in Toronto, where she met my children. Later, my son Rupert, who must have been three or four at the time, told me that she had taught him a German rhyme, which he still remembers:

*Ich bau, ich bau ein steinern Haus*
*vorne guckt ein Esel raus*
*hinten eine Kuh*
*Muh!*

[I build, I build a house of stone.
In front a donkey peeks out,
In the back, a cow:
Moo!]

A confined *Selbstgefühl* if ever there was one.

# Five Poems

## KIT FAN

## Raw Materials

**Day 1**
a friend of a
friend is
shuffled out
of a radio
show.
Another
mouth shut.
Another
man's
whereabouts
unknown.
His dual-
nationality
scrapped.

**Day 2**
a bookseller's
accused of
crowdfunding
a protest.
Evidence of
systematic
failure
destroyed.
Burberry is
boycotted by
some stars.
Government
tells fourteen
countries to
deny the
legality of a
passport.

**Day 3**
a law firm is
ordered to
disband
because they
defend a case.
A university
axes a photo
exhibition.

**Day 4**
someone
suspends a
talk show,
someone
cancels a
documentary,
someone bans
the Oscars,
someone
restricts
someone's
access to
something
official.

**Day 5**
another man is
heard and
charged. A law
amended.
Police
empowered.
Election
candidates
screened.

## Mnemosyne
### *for Mimi Ching*

**found her in Mong Kok**
throwing herself into
the pepper smoke
*lacrimae lacrimae*

**a million footsteps shaped**
the water movement
as guns followed the eyes
of cameras

**they split**
as the blue-dyed rain
stained the running
feet the kneeling feet

**resist and keep**
the city in the sovereign
present in the foreign
tongue

**can't choose between**
the goddess of memory
and forgetting which is
the alpha privative of thought

**hunt him down find**
him again on WhatsApp
hospital wards inside
tunnels over bridges

**do you ever think of**
me a blind spot a thorn
on your side a disremembered
joint declaration

**not like flesh**
and blood not like
immortalised slogans
on Lennon Walls

**between flames and sirens**
under shield and batons
which sheep from the flock
would you remove

bound to be here
in the divided capital
of capital in the sticky
heat of chaos

dear friend why on earth
you jumped into the clouds
what worlds were there
to encode

## After the Quake

11th November 1855, 10 p.m.

The black-haired clouds that choked
the mouth of Arakawa River
weren't clouds. And the grey stubble

that grew on the morning snow
in the rice fields
wasn't only dead skin. The kids smothered

soot into their lampblack eyes
though footprints, a whole town of them,
had been eaten by the crows

that weren't crows. New names jostled
their way onto the crowded
noticeboard. And snow landed on the ink

dissolving.  I didn't know what the bone-
coloured sky wanted but it kept begging me
to read it.

24th August 2016, 3:36 a.m.

It was your birthday. We kissed each other
good night.  A dog barked and shook the lamp.
I turned off, left Aleppo behind with its limbs.
We slept with our heads elsewhere.

I woke and called the noise a ghost. You woke.
It threw us out of bed, naked. We crawled
under the IKEA table. Two wine glasses broke.
The ceiling fidgeted as the ground force mauled

the night for 30 seconds. We took our passports
to the open square. Sleepy kids in shorts
dozed like walnuts in their mothers' hands.
Men smoked busily by the newsstands.

After an hour we went back upstairs
and shut the door. It returned, but milder.
We lay in bed like stemless sunflowers.
A dog barked and we kissed each other.

## The Art of Descent

I don't know why
  after years of separation
    her fear of descent

into the world under
  still presses at my heels
    as if underness

  is a lake of vantablack
    ink everyone will plunge in
      get stained by

  and forget about living
    risks and defects
      like I'm doing now

  stealing the day from a climb
    up Easedale Tarn having dipped
      into the ice-water

    butt-naked as two buzzards
      patrolled the sun-clipped
        crags like cats

    bringing in a small creature
      at the edge of
      breath

    Mother
      unlike you who fell down
        two flights of stairs

      and lost your brain
        to decades of migraine
          I'm well and taking my time

      held by my beloved
        accompanied by friends on this steep
        narrow path

      where each step
        grows firmer when my desire
          to balance loses foothold

      and time morphs
        into muscles and waters
          as we keep looking back

      but fail to translate what
        gravity and friction do
          to the stream

      making these stable
        repeatable braids that knot
        and unknot

      on the surface
        while I can't stop blinking and thinking
        with Orpheus

## What You Look Like

Like courtroom sketches of the accused
devoid of all expression
your lipid membrane looks as lifeless
as the dark side of the moon
your spike glycoprotein red as roses
nimble as hands though electron-microscopically
speaking they aren't scarlet or vermilion
nothing to do with blood or lust
coronas or aggression but two interlocking
sub-units like a labyrinth of knitted wool
with endings and openings that give
your unmistakable binding grip
but also make you vulnerable
not unlike the flaws our maker forgot
when reproducing his own image
while in the background of the newsroom
sometimes you look like Yayoi Kusama's
infinite polka dots and sometimes like
Kandinsky's unfinished circles in boxes
or Seurat's pointillistic calm stolen from
the grey smoke and chimneys on the horizon
which still looks like our own horizon now
and although nothing any longer is impossible
with Athena's shield and spear
for months I've failed to commit your portrait
to memory as if what you look like is not
what you really look like when people
describe you generically as almond-eyed
with creaseless lids
bespectacled
black haired
funny nosed
masked
foreign

# Two Poems

## STAV POLEG

### Absolute Scenes
*After Dante's Purgatorio*

*non sapei tu che qui è l'uom felice?*

London, spring equinox. There are absolute scenes
in the airport leading towards this dream. The ceiling is tilting,
turning into the floor. It's snowing in here so I'm pressing
the skylight into the blue-icy fog and look – in the distance –
a ship trying the sapphire-green sea like an incomplete
thought – beautiful – a star forms in the dark like a small provocation,
and three more! The sky, an unsettled machine. Look, I'm now deep
in season two of *A Kind of Middle Point.* Can we call it that? A kind
of middle point – time according to Aristotle (Physics) or the point
between deficiency and excess (Ethics) and, yes – what the hell
is going on? So many questions – the girl driving a car
in the rain instead of a poem, is she heading towards or leaving
the cliffs hanging over the sea? May I say how I love
the title song: *England, an Invitation.*

England, an invitation in the form of a lingua-franca
machine, a strong sense of failure and as good a place as any
for 'What are writers for?' Dear reader, pick up a stick, circle
the false answer: for climbing steep, spherical
islands / turning ice into sapphire-blue fields / playing
poets *and* the main characters / taking dreams literally, trains
symbolically / trying out physics and ethics / getting lost
in the middle of things / misreading subject for matter / choice
for free-will. Here in the city of reconfiguration, let me
offer you a Pop Art green apple, an island as mountain
and a time-bending machine. Now, as the hour of sea-surfers
carries longing like prayer – a recurring
short film – dear dreamer, fasten your seatbelt
as we gear up for language, I mean landing, I mean, I mean,

Language, I mean landing, I mean, I mean –
all day on the train to King's Cross I'm running in Dante
towards the gate, the two flickering locks, the precarious point
where Purgatorio begins. Dear runner, my fellow newcomer –
how is time working for you? How is longing? Years of practice
and I'm still failing in both. So instead, I'll be trying
to draw characters into this land, I mean story, the way a thought
could lift the shadow of Ulysses from the eighth circle
of Hell to the siren catching his name on this steep-terrace
walk. Here, on the cliff of show-off and hunger, here
on the Circle Line platform towards Liverpool Street, take the keys
to that thing you have split into unequal halves and named
talent and discipline – dear runner, you who are always
a newcomer in another wild scene – open the gates.

In another wild scene – open the gates. London,
send your ships and fast-flying machines, take me to the shores
of Tate Modern's turbine hall and concrete pyramid and a 'Fellini
Celebration' at the BFI – yay! (There are so many staircases
in *La Dolce Vita*, so many spirals, exits, uprooted sculptors
and ceilings, ruined and locked doors.) Remember, reader, the river
caught in the night like a question, the Northern Line pulsing
new fog, the girl climbing up the down escalator, eager
to miss the train home – her bag falling, keys, books, her phone gliding
towards the floor? Midway upon running in Dante I have reached
the Terrace of Wrath. Here in the land of overground circles
and high-altitude cranes, here where a thought is as solid and real
as the matter that wrestles with it until it takes form – *And you
have a mind that planets cannot rule or stars concern.*

*A mind that planets cannot rule or stars concern* – a thing so
real it turns matter to more matter, more stairways and bridges, more
air. And you have a city you're trying to rein – an image, a word –
shall we go over the plan? The night as vacant cathedral / train
station? Yes. The fully conceived Negroni Sbagliato? Ma certo!
Getting lost on the terrace of wrath? Dear reader, I'm here, running
in Dante all night at King's Cross. And what about time, matter,
space? I'm thinking of Peter Brook's, *with a cut the mind
can flick from yesterday to Australia* – here in the city
of theatre makers, shall we go into that? As for vice versus
sin – vice as the Aristotelian take – a tendency for wrongdoing
rather than definite, absolute sin – a different kind of losing
direction – higher and deeper and so full of change – dear Dante –
dear poet and protagonist – plug this into my vein.

Plug this into my vein: the river, the fire, the three
poets climbing towards a towering forest – a different
kind of losing direction, the clearest-blue air. As for hunger
and why the shades in this place still experience
it – as for pain – since climbing this rock has always involved
some kind of prayer, poetry, unsettled scripts, I'll be going for
Wittgenstein: *You learned the concept 'pain' in learning
language.* You learned the concept of absence by uttering
a name. Three times Virgil is called – three times
he drifts further away. Here, where your own loss is part
of an always much greater anarchy, here where the night carries
sunsets and dawns like recurring-dark questions:
*How were you able to ascend the mountain? Did you not know
that man is happy here?* England, an invitation.

England, an invitation – a different kind of losing
direction – bigger and far greater on the unruly threshold
of season three. Dear runner, if you struggle to handle the angels
wielding seven candelabras, the air – blue with cold fire, the four
creatures each with six wings, or those wild, wild visions
of the apocalypse, remember this – you may drive down
in circles all the way back to the terrace of wrath – a kind
of middle point. I'll be here, back in canto sixteen, studying
the wounds that can burn in the dark across language and
matter, I mean – time. Longing, hunger, the velocity
of loss – *you who are free are subjects* – at what point
does a city turn into one's own subject and matter, the language
you carry and care for, the streets you're running and trying
to dream? London, spring equinox, there are absolute scenes.

# The Letter

Think of it as an installation –
on a glass table, a ceramic-blue
plate – an invitation –

margarita on ice, a hand reaching
for an orange segment, perhaps
it is summer, the changing

of weather. Perhaps you've just
got off the train. The sky like a boy playing
with sunset – you don't know

how it happened, you don't have to
explain. The street is a sunflower
field. The sea, an ongoing

question. Some things
are like this – the traffic, the trees –
an aesthetic dispute – an oscillation –

and far off – the forest
of uneven streets – a karaoke bar
pulsing heat and new

weather. How the light
takes hold of the traffic, the river's dark
floor. How the dark travels

upwards – the coal-silver stars
like a far-off vacation, the inconsistency
of a moon crescent – you know

how it works – it's midsummer, the distance
of stars moving further, the rain
coming in

like a fine stage-direction. Think of it
as a study in pain against
language – the river, the trees –

there's always a thought moving
closer, an unscheduled thunder, a storm
in a picture you're still holding

close. I have to admit – I didn't expect
to see you this early, carrying
a letter – the same one

you tore into pieces years and countries
ago. I think what happened
is this –

you must have managed
to go back in time. Time? Think of it
as a provocation–

a yellow leaf caught in blue-bicycle
weather, a train testing distance
with an inaccurate

question, an equation of words against
speed. It's been raining all day but look –
you have managed to draw your way

here. There are so many windows
in the towering building over the bridge
but only one window

is lit with waves of blue and dark
green. Think of it as a repetition –
on the seventh floor

a woman is watching the same film
she's never able to watch. Some things
are too close, and how often

they move even closer
in films. But this evening, as the rain
plays with darkness across the landscape

of streets, she's leaning against
the half-open window, running a thought
at full speed. The moon –

a recurring wrong
question. The street, a loose
string. Perhaps you've been running for days

in this weather. Perhaps you've just
got off the train. And yes,
there was never

a letter, only a chamber – the movement
of words against words. You don't have
to explain. Some letters

open and close
like an unwritten rumour
but they matter, they matter. How else

would you walk in this wide field
of thought – the moon as a hot-air balloon,
the night – a train

station. You don't know
how it happens. You don't know
how it happens.

# *from* NB by JC

## A walk through the *Times Literary Supplement*

### JAMES CAMPBELL

*March 23, 2001*

Anyone nursing a rejection slip is likely to feel better after perusing the current issue of the *Missouri Review*. The latest in its 'Found Text' series is a feature on readers' reports from the archives of the publisher Alfred A. Knopf. The list of rejectees is spectacular, and the comments are frank. In 1949, for example, a reader recommended turning down a collection of stories by Jorge Luis Borges, *El Aleph*, with the comment 'they are utterly untranslatable, at least into anything that could be expected to sell more than 750 copies'. The reader himself found the stories 'remarkable', but thought they would appear to the general public as '$50-a-pound caviar'. *El Aleph* would not be translated for another twenty-one years.

Anaïs Nin was felt to be 'a small, arbitrary, overpraised talent who has been able to hide her emptiness behind a lot of chinoiserie', and *A Spy in the House of Love*, later a Penguin Classic, was kicked out. In 1953, the young Peter Matthiessen submitted 'a very bad novel' called *Signs of Winter*. 'We had great hopes for this guy', sighed the reader, before stamping 'REJECT'. The title has never seen the light of day. Two years later, Knopf saw off Italo Calvino, with reluctance, and the young James Baldwin, without it. *Giovanni's Room* merited extended comment, as Baldwin had published a promising debut novel with the firm in 1953. The novel seemed to the first reader 'an unhappy, talented, and repellent book', to the second 'a bleak little tale', and to the third 'hopelessly bad'. 'We must try to persuade him to put this away; it will do neither publisher nor author any good. It will have bad reviews and bad sales.'

Sales to date have probably topped the million mark.

In 1956, it was the turn of *Lolita* ('impossible for us'), followed by a novel by John Barth ('I cannot conceive of a healthy mind producing this'), Isaac Bashevis Singer ('not worth Knopf's time and effort'), an apprentice Joyce Carol Oates ('for all I know the long-hairs may single this out as a masterpiece... but it is incomprehensible'). Sylvia Plath's novel *The Bell Jar* got a similar reception – 'ill-conceived, poorly written, occasionally atrocious' – as did Jean Rhys's *Wide Sargasso Sea* and *The Joke* by Milan Kundera. The last was found to be 'a long sentimental wail'. Knopf published later novels by Kundera.

Apart from their entertainment value, the reports give an intimate glimpse of the times in which they were written. Knopf readers no longer write reports.

*April 13, 2001*

Carrie Kipling, Rudyard's wife, was 'one of the most loathed women of her generation', according to a new book about her. It is also reported there that Henry James called her 'this hard capable little person'. You may be wondering how it is possible to gauge degrees of loathing for an entire generation; you may even be aware that what James said was 'this hard, devoted, capable little person' – somewhat different – but only a pedant would want to spoil good hype.

The book in question, by Adam Nicolson, is part of a new series, Short Lives, published by Short Books. The ninety-six-page Life of the devoted and capable Carrie is called *The Hated Wife*. On the back cover, Nicci Gerrard, the *Observer* journalist, joins in: 'Adam Nicolson takes Mrs Kipling – for so long despised – and gives her back her humanity.' Hated, loathed, despised? Well, you say, at least Carrie had the consolation of being married to a great man. Wrong again. 'It was she who provided the backbone that her husband privately lacked.'

Even Mr Nicolson acknowledges that Carrie Kipling could be awkward. Her sister-in-law Mai, as well as certain friends, 'thought there was something mad about Carrie'. She was jealous of Mai's beauty, and as a result, Mr Nicolson says, was apt to 'patronize' her. She suspected her brother of cheating her financially, and treated him 'with a miserliness which any man would have resented'. But the time of the great writer's wife has come – Fanny Stevenson, Frieda Lawrence, Nora Joyce, Vivienne Eliot, Zelda Fitzgerald and others have been receiving their rewards at last. There is no reason to leave Carrie behind.

As part of the process, the great writer himself must undergo revision. Not only did Kipling lack backbone, he was secretly queer. 'It was not Carrie with whom Kipling fell in love', Mr Nicolson writes, 'but her brother Wolcott.' Does he mean that the two men were lovers? 'The way in which, in later life, Kipling wrote and spoke with such frantic loathing of homosexuality as a beastly and bestial business has been taken as a sign that they were.' It couldn't, by any chance, be a sign that they weren't?

*August 22, 2003*

If you study at the University of Colorado, Boulder, you might benefit from the teaching of Frederick Luis Aldama, Assistant Professor of English. Mr Aldama's new book, *Postethnic Narrative Criticism* deals with the work of Salman Rushdie, Hanif Kureishi, Oscar Acosta and other writers. Dig that postethnic rhythm: 'The Acosta-as-character's hypervisibility as abnormal / unreal ethnosexual object ironically leads him into an empowered ethnosexual position that playfully resists hegemonic structures.' The chapter on Rushdie is equally playful:

Rushdie's magicorealism gives texture to a culturally

and racially complex and comprehensive fourthspace; rather than invent story-worlds and narrators that reproduce a binary opposition between a firstspace – coded as racial Other, prerational, magical – Rushdie uses magicorealism as the form to invent fourthspace narratives that critically revise such divisions.

But hold on there. It's time to stop mocking this kind of thing, and to ask what tragedies have befallen the Aldamas of academe to have caused their minds to melt. We were just getting into our new compassionate mode when we read the preface to Aldama's book – and there discovered that his misfortune is all our fault. The author tells us that, as a boy in the 1980s, he journeyed 'far from my Mexican / Guatemalan-American family' and arrived in London, a city 'filled to the brim with Marmite-eating xenophobes'. His sojourn 'coincided with Mrs Thatcher's reign of terror'. The Prime Minister had begun 'to "sweep up" Britain's impure Others... council flats were levelled and the urban poor displaced'. When young Aldama and other Others 'wandered too deeply into London's moneyed West End, police would inform us of a city curfew and escort us to the nearest underground station'.

Distracted by reigns of terror in Chile, Uganda, Cambodia, not to mention the social upheavals in parts of Mexico and Guatemala, we missed our own. Things have picked up, though. The Marmite-eaters are in retreat, the moneyed West End curfew has been lifted. As for the displaced urban poor, they are in place again, and numerous enough to please even an Assistant Professor. Come back, Mr Aldama. Let us help you learn to write the English of the new impurity.

### January 5, 2007

Where are the poets of the war? This was the question posed in a leading article in the *TLS* of August 8, 1942, when Britain and other nations were three years into the struggle against Germany. The leader writer contrasted the current situation with that of 'the last war' which 'threw up a fair amount of notable poetry'. To the names of soldier-poets from the First World War, such as Owen, Graves, Sassoon, Brooke and Rosenberg, could be added Kipling, Bridges, Hardy and others who were 'not soldiers', but who viewed the conflict 'through the accumulated knowledge and wisdom of years'. Indeed, our editorialist said, 'the singers of war have been for the most part not soldiers', even though the poetry of Europe is 'full of war'.

We have now been at war for over five years, first in Afghanistan, then Iraq. Where are the poets of the war? We exclude, for the moment, poems gathered together in collections such as *100 Poets Against the War*, edited by Todd Swift, and *101 Poets Against War*, edited by Matthew Hollis and Paul Keegan, the very titles of which amount to a political agenda (the former contained new work; the latter, poems from all ages). The kind of war poetry you want, as a reader, challenges your assumptions with doubt, pity, glory, even gore.

Our most distinguished living war poet is probably Christopher Logue, but his *War Music*, a wonderful modernist assembly kit based on a selective chart of the *Iliad*, can only be applied to the present situation in the sense

that practically anything can. Under no reading could it be classed as anti-war. James Fenton has written about a previous war; Seamus Heaney and others have addressed themselves to the Troubles in Northern Ireland (at least one poem in Heaney's latest collection glances in the direction of Afghanistan). But no writer of distinction has borne down on the wars in Afghanistan and Iraq with the authority of direct experience and few, if any, with 'the accumulated knowledge and wisdom of the years'. An exception might be Harold Pinter. No writer has ever been so belligerent about belligerence.

One explanation for the paucity of war poetry lies in the ending of National Service. Another in the present-day unfashionable standing of nationalism and militarism. 'Is there no such thing as righteous indignation?' our editorialist wrote in 1942. 'May not a dear homeland be in imminent danger?'

As it turned out, the Second World War threw up 'a fair amount of notable poetry' by Keith Douglas, Sydney Keyes, Alan Ross and others. In 1942, they appeared to our leader writer as the reserves (the first two were killed; the third seriously wounded). Yet he conceded that war had given them that much-desired thing, a subject. 'Were there no war, they would still be poets, but poets compelled, like all children of this age, to think, observe, and write within a narrow living-space.'

### February 8, 2008

How senior politicians find the time to write, while shouldering the burdens of office, is a mystery to us all. Take Gordon Brown, for example. Since September 2006, he has published three books, two of them since becoming Prime Minister: *Courage: Eight portraits*; *Britain's Everyday Heroes*; and *Moving Britain Forward: Speeches*. These are added to his existing bibliography, which includes biographies of the socialist MPs James Maxton and Keir Hardie.

Mr Brown has also contributed to other people's books. Readers of the *TLS* of January 18 may recall the review of several studies of the great economist Adam Smith, one of which, *Adam Smith, Radical and Egalitarian* by Iain McLean, came with a foreword 'written specially' by the Prime Minister. Our reviewer, Richard Bourke, quoted a sentence from the introduction: 'Coming from Kirkcaldy as Adam Smith did, I have come to understand that his *Wealth of Nations* was underpinned by his *Theory of Moral Sentiments*.' Mr Bourke pondered this, and wondered 'how exactly has coming from Kirkcaldy enabled the Prime Minister to arrive at his understanding?' Mr Brown's introduction then indulged in some fine feeling about Adam Smith's civic virtue and 'neighbourliness', which left Mr Bourke, a senior lecturer in history at the University of London, unimpressed.

This curious claim to intuitive geographical sympathy rang a bell. In December 2005, Mr Brown delivered the Hugo Young memorial lecture at Chatham House, London, in which he said: 'Coming from Kirkcaldy as Adam Smith did, I have come to understand that his *Wealth of Nations* was underpinned by his *Theory of Moral Sentiments*.'

The Prime Minister has now written an introduction to the first British edition of *The Roads to Modernity* by

Gertrude Himmelfarb, which tackles 'such thinkers as Adam Smith, David Hume and Edmund Burke'. First Brown tells us that 'the British Enlightenment' was 'not just the province of the privileged', but was, in New Labour style, 'accessible to all'. He then writes: 'Coming from Kirkcaldy as Adam Smith did, I have come to understand that his *Wealth of Nations* was underpinned by his *Theory of Moral Sentiments*.' There follows some fine feeling about civic virtue and 'neighbourliness'. Having two arms and two legs, as George Santayana did, we have come to understand that those who do not remember their own waffle are condemned to repeat it.

### June 20, 2008

Writing in the *Guardian Review* last month, the novelist Hilary Mantel recalled her life in Botswana in 1978. The country had one road, no television, and little in the way of a free press. Ms Mantel 'subscribed to the *TLS*, which came late after many overland adventures'. The investment might appear sensible, but Ms Mantel found it 'hardly a publication to get you excited'. For what seemed to her 'like months' during that year, the letters columns 'were dominated by a fraught, increasingly savage set of exchanges about Gray's *Elegy*'. The correspondence 'centred on the line "And drowsy tinklings lull the distant folds", which – some lamented – Gray wouldn't have written if he had been less ignorant about sheep farming'.

Unlike Ms Mantel, we find the idea of an exchange on eighteenth-century sheep farming a diverting prospect. When we rummaged the *TLS* index for 1978 in search of Thomas Gray, however, we drew a blank. Nor is there any reference to the poet or his *Elegy* in 1979. We did find a well-informed piece about the manuscript of the poem in the issue of May 27, 1977, but there is not a word in it about sheep farming, and not a single savage reader wrote in response.

Now there has landed on our desk something to get Ms Mantel properly excited: *Elegy in a Country Churchyard: Latin translations*, a collection of forty-five versions of Gray's poem, starting in 1762, eleven years after its original publication, concluding with that of Donald Gibson, one of the book's editors, made in 2001.

The opening lines of the *Elegy* are among the best-known in English poetry:

The curfew tolls the knell of parting day,
The lowing herd winds slowly o'er the lea,
The ploughman homeward plods his weary way,
And leaves the world to darkness and to me.

Robert Langrishe's version, made in 1775, takes an enjoyably straightforward approach:

Vespertina notat finem campana diei,
Pigra armenta boant, tarde tenduntque per agros,
Passibus erga domum lassis se vertit arator,
Et totas terras tenebrisque mihique relinquit.

As for the line mysteriously engraved in Ms Mantel's memory – 'And drowsy tinklings lull the distant folds' – Langrishe offers 'Tinnitus ad somnum pecudes ducitque soporans', which even she might think neat and to the point.

For music, as well as meaning, Langrishe's rendering of the famous opening beats many others. John Wright (1786) gives us the tongue-twisting 'Triste dat occidui signum campana diei', while William Woty (1789) offers just as much of a mouthful, with 'Decessum graviter pulsat Campana diei'. Henry Latham's 1864 attempt seems positively discordant: 'Jam campana diem morituram plangit'. Latham's rendering of the drowsy tinklings – 'aut qua / Languescente procul tinnit ovile sono' – likewise misses the soporific substance, his daring caesura notwithstanding.

Our hope is that these samplings will inspire Ms Mantel to recall the real name of the journal in which she read the savage exchanges, and that she will pass it on. No one should have cause to think her one 'in aeternum se ad muta oblivia tradens' – or to turn from Langrishe's eloquent rendering back to the original, 'to dumb forgetfulness a prey'.

### January 23, 2009

To who it may concern: In a letter published in the *Guardian* (January 17), headed 'Whom is doomed', the children's author Michael Rosen rebuked an earlier letter writer, Andrew Papworth, for insisting on the correct use of whom. The paper's error occurred in a headline, which read: 'Signed, sealed, delivered: by who?' Mr Papworth described this as poor usage. Mr Rosen objected: 'It could only have been called "poor" if the usage had created difficulties for the reader... Neither the *Guardian* nor anyone else should let themselves be cowed by the grammar bullies.'

In Mr Papworth's eyes, the headline-writer appeared to be a person in who he had no trust, to who he would not entrust his journalistic copy, for who he would not write nothing. Far be it from we to wag the fingers at Mr Rosen. His point – no usage is 'poor' that makes itself understood – is common enough, and neglects the advantages of style and elegance. If writers theirselves are heard declaring that it doesn't matter what you write, only that you are understood, then we feel impelled to put a fight up. Ask not who the bell tolls for, Mr Rosen, it tolls for thou.

### February 17, 2012

February 14 will henceforth be known as Saint Jeanette's Day. Fresh from having issued a 250-page public shaming of her adoptive mother, Jeanette Winterson is 'optimistic about love again':

love in every shape and size and disguise. Known love, new love, love's ghosts, love's hopes... Love is an ecosystem. You can't neglect it, exploit it, pollute it, and wonder what happened to the birds and the bees.

With money 'gone' – 'it was an illusion' – there is an opportunity to 're-think love'.

Once a child preacher in Accrington, Lancashire, Jeanette has never ceased quoting from the Book of Jeanette. No other contemporary writer would get away with it – imagine Julian Barnes instructing us to 're-think love' – but for some reason she does. The *Guardian* gave up its front page on February 14, for Jeanette to say, 'hug those who love us – and give some hugs to those who don't get loved enough'. And to say it again: 'Love your loved ones. Love the stranger.'

There was something for every member of the flock. If 'love is an ecosystem' has you re-thinking just that bit too much, try 'There are so many different kinds of love', or 'Love is an alternative currency.' Or, indeed, 'Children need so much love.' Teenagers were not forgotten. 'They need to see that love can change and deepen.' Think about it, then re-think about it. Money is an illusion, but 'love isn't a commodity'.

'We all had a fantasy that love could take care of itself.' We did, didn't we all? Now let's make the planet 'a place we can call home'. Love your loved ones. (Saint Jeanette didn't re-think that one through.) The piece will remain on the website until April 1, when the *Guardian* will take it down.

### October 5, 2012

When travelling, Drummond Moir copies the wording of signs in hotels: 'To call a broad from France, first dial 00.' 'Please leave your values at the front desk.' 'French widow in every room.' He has seen an advertisement for Dickens's fifth novel, 'Barney, by Rudge', read in a newspaper that 'Bishops Agree Sex Abuse Rules' and enjoyed a government report that promised, 'There can be no scared cows'. A notice in his car park assures drivers: 'Illegally parked cars will be fine.' All find their way into *Just My Typo*.

Among the most enjoyable is the metatypo, such as the deferential erratum from the *Dublin Journal*: 'In our last issue: for His Grace the Duchess of Dorset, read Her Grace, the Duke of Dorset.' Punctuation is all, as station sign-writers know: 'Passengers must stay with their luggage at all times or they will be taken away and destroyed.' Who will argue with the slogan of the well-known insurance firm: 'Prudential – were there to help you'?

Did Fox News really broadcast the bulletin, 'Obama Bin Laden is dead'? Did an anti-immigration group carry a sign that said 'Respect Are Country: Read English'. And while it is delightful to think of the church choir congregating for evening sinning practice, we do wonder. Never mind. As an 1864 edition of the Bible suggested, 'Rejoice and be exceedingly clad!'

### January 11, 2013

About once a year, there is a mini-debate about the timidity of book reviewing. It has been going on for some time. 'Sweet, bland commendations fall everywhere upon the scene; a universal, if somewhat lobotomized, accommodation reigns.' That was Elizabeth Hardwick, in 1959. More recently, a writer in the online journal *Slate* suggested that the blogging, tweeting free-for-all that sometimes passes for criticism fosters too much 'niceness', not necessarily a nice quality.

To halt the saccharine spread, the not-so nice sharpened their tools and carved out the Hatchet Job of the Year. The first award went to Adam Mars-Jones, for a review of Michael Cunningham's book *By Nightfall*, and the shortlist for the second has been announced. There are eight nominations, including Richard Evans's review of A.N. Wilson's *Hitler* ('It's hard to think why a publishing house that once had a respected history list agreed to produce this travesty'; *New Statesman*), Claire Harman on *Silver: A return to Treasure Island* by Andrew Motion ('at every turn the former Poet Laureate clogs the works with verbiage'; *Evening Standard*), Allan Massie on Craig Raine's novel *The Divine Comedy* ('some of the writing is very bad'; *Scotsman*), Camilla Long on Rachel Cusk's story of her marriage break-up, *Aftermath* ('quite simply, bizarre... acres of poetic whimsy and vague literary blah'; *Sunday Times*) and Ron Charles on Martin Amis's 'ham-fisted' *Lionel Asbo* (*Washington Post*).

The favourite is likely to be the review by Zoë Heller of Salman Rushdie's memoir *Joseph Anton*, which appeared in the *New York Review of Books* last month. One commentator had already relished it as 'a hatchet job among hatchet jobs'; another welcomed the 'most pointedly brutal review' of 2012.

Brutality is never nice. Enjoying a healthy demolition as much as anyone, however, we reached for Ms Heller's piece with a certain shameful anticipation – only to discover that it is thoughtful and well-written, not in the least brutal; on a par with the excellent review of Rushdie's book in the *TLS* by Eric Ormsby. Hatchet-job prizes are good fun (not so much for Rushdie, Cusk and others) but it would be unfortunate if critics felt they were being urged to draw blood, to show off their 'sharp' edge. The reviewer's chief responsibility is to the potential purchaser of the book, who, unlike the remunerated reviewer, is asked to pay hard-earned cash for the product. The most difficult task for a reviewer is to remain true in writing to the feelings experienced while reading, to convey them in elegant, entertaining prose. It's tougher than being brutal.

### October 4, 2012

Picking up a glossy Penguin edition of Graham Greene's novel *Brighton Rock* in a friend's house the other day, we read on the cover that it is 'Now a Major Motion Picture'. Is it? Was it 'major' even in 2010 when the film in question appeared, with Helen Mirren in the role of Ida (not to be confused with the Boulting brothers' 1947 version)? We have a vague memory of its release, thanks to the disproportionate amount of publicity movies attract when a household name is in the cast. One of five films Ms Mirren made that year, it disappeared almost immediately, on the back of weary reviews.

What is a major film? *Casablanca*, maybe; *City Lights*; *High Noon*; *Vertigo*; *8½*; *The Battle of Algiers*; *Les 400 Coups*; *The Bill Douglas Trilogy*. Throw in something by Bergman. Everyone has their own ideas and their own list. We successfully avoided the latest screen version of *Brighton Rock*. The cover image on the unhappy Penguin of Sam Riley, who played Pinkie, compounded by an inane foreword by the screenwriter Rowan Joffe, put us off rereading the novel. We have never heard anyone mention the film in conversation, even to say they disliked it. What's the 'major' bit?

A new edition of William Faulkner's novel *As I Lay Dying* has just been issued, with a picture of the actor (and director) James Franco on the cover, and the same legend, 'Now a Major Motion Picture'. It drew criticism from pro-Faulknerians and anti-Francoites, countered by the familiar philistine response: 'If this causes a single kid in high school to pick up Faulkner's novel, then the film will have done its job.'

*As I Lay Dying* is, in fact, officially a minor motion picture. The *Huffington Post* reported this week that 'James Franco's adaptation of *As I Lay Dying* was scheduled for a Sept 27 theatrical debut. Days before the film was set to arrive in theaters, however, it was announced that it will not be shown on the big screen.' The distributor, Millennium Films, plans to release Franco's *As I Lay Dying* on October 22, on iTunes.

At the end of August, a brick-sized copy of *Salinger*, edited by David Shields and Shane Salerno, arrived, bearing a self-directed compliment on the cover: 'The Official Book of the Acclaimed Documentary Film'. That'll be the acclaimed film that had yet to be released when the book came out? The acclaimed film that was panned when it appeared last month? If Salerno and Shields cause one kid in high school… then who cares what fictions they come up with?

### November 27, 2015

*Carol*, directed by Todd Haynes and starring Cate Blanchett, may or may not be a stimulating film, but it is based on one of the dullest of Patricia Highsmith's twenty-two novels. At its best, Highsmith's intrigue derives from the guilty thoughts of an innocent person, and the clear conscience of a guilty one. There is no crime in *Carol*; just a repetitious story of two women in love.

Originally called *The Price of Salt* (1952), *Carol* was Highsmith's second book. That she herself knew the mode was not for her is suggested by the fact that she published it under the name Claire Morgan. Forgotten for decades, *Carol* is currently being acclaimed as a classic. 'It soon chalked up a million copies', Jill Dawson wrote in the *Guardian* in May, referring to the Bantam paperback of 1953 – an implausible figure, now repeated whenever the novel is mentioned. You will find it on Wikipedia, for example (source: 'Dawson, Jill, *Guardian*, May 13, 2015'). Ms Dawson's own source is likely to be Highsmith, who claimed in the afterword to the 1991 reissue of *Carol* – the first to use her real name – that the 1953 edition sold 'nearly a million'. That's already a reduction. A Bantam paperback from 1969 estimates 'over half a million copies in print'.

Million-selling or even half-million-selling books were as rare then as they are now. The initial print run for one of the biggest books of 1952, *The Old Man and the Sea*, was 50,000 copies and we may assume that Steinbeck's *East of Eden* had a similar production, though both books sold many times that figure as their reputations grew. That year's Mickey Spillane (*Kiss Me Deadly*) might have sold half a million.

There are now several editions of *Carol* to choose from, including one issued by Norton under the original title. On the cover, we read: 'The novel that inspired *Lolita*' – a contentious claim and one that would have baffled Vladimir Nabokov. Where did it come from? In Volume Two of Brian Boyd's comprehensive biography of Nabokov (*The American Years*), there is a mention of

Carroll, Lewis, but none of *Carol*, or of Highsmith, Patricia. The source is likely to be an article by Terry Castle, Professor of Humanities at Stanford, published in the *New Republic* in 2003. 'I have long had a theory that Nabokov knew *The Price of Salt*, and modelled the climactic cross-country car chase in *Lolita* on Therese and Carol's frenzied bid for freedom.'

You can have theories about whatever you choose, but this one hasn't got much going for it: Nabokov began writing *Lolita* in 1949; by the time *The Price of Salt* appeared, his novel was largely complete. It is likely he never heard of 'Claire Morgan', before or after. We have a theory that Ms Castle doesn't know *Lolita*'s publication history: in a second piece on the subject (*Slate*, May 23, 2006), she gives the date of the first edition as 1958, three years late.

You can say anything you like about Highsmith these days, as long as it fits the project. Phyllis Nagy, who wrote the screenplay of *Carol*, told the *Guardian* that Highsmith found *Plein Soleil* – the 1960 French adaptation of *The Talented Mr Ripley* – 'ridiculous', even though it is well established that its star, Alain Delon, was her favourite Ripley. As for the film of *Carol*, Nagy is confident that Highsmith 'would have finally thought we've got something'.

We have another theory: it's safer, on the whole, to stay at home and read *The Cry of the Owl*, *The Tremor of Forgery*, *This Sweet Sickness*, *Deep Water* or any of the Ripleys.

### September 2, 2016

Do you read reviews of your books? We never do. We're in good company. Asked by an audience member at an event how she felt about the poor reception of her latest, *In Other Words*, Jhumpa Lahiri 'fell silent, pursing her lips… 'I don't read reviews', she said.' Jeanette Winterson doesn't read them, 'because by then it's too late – whatever anyone says, the book won't change'. A. L. Kennedy leaves it to her publisher to 'tell me how they're going'. Not only can John Banville not read reviews of his books, he can't stand the books themselves. 'They are an embarrassment to me', he told the *Irish Independent*. The Scottish novelist Ronald Frame isn't reviewed as much as he once was, but he won't have noticed. 'The reviews, I was told, were welcoming', he said of *Havisham* (2014). 'I never read my reviews – truly!'

Ian McEwan is the same. His new novel, *Nutshell*, is released this week. In a *Guardian* interview, he admitted that he expects the reviews to be 'wildly varied', but naturally he won't be reading them. His wife provides edited summaries, steering clear of the worst ones. When he happened to see that 'some troll-like person on the *Spectator*' had declared his previous novel, *The Children Act*, to be 'unforgivably bad', he simply 'had to turn my head away'. At the same time, he claims, unconvincingly, that it made him smile. Not only him. 'When I told Julian Barnes, he fell about laughing. I mean, how bad can I get?'

Or how unobservant? We have the *Spectator* review to hand. It begins by stating that *The Children Act* 'could hardly be more attuned to the temper of the times' and ends by comparing it to James Joyce's long story 'The

Dead'. Not bad. In between, the writing is judged 'lazy' and the plot development 'improbable'; but the phrase 'unforgivably bad' is not there.

The 'troll-like' reviewer – troll-like in the Nordic sense or in the computerish way? – was Cressida Connolly, daughter of the celebrated critic Cyril. She has written books of her own, including one about happy childhoods. On the basis of a single encounter many years ago, she seemed to us as untroll-like a figure as it is possible to be (in either sense). The sole appearance of the word 'unforgivable' in the *Spectator* review of *The Children Act* is in the headline, and it isn't linked with 'bad'. So wind back the film, Mr McEwan. Let Julian Barnes rise up from his fallen-about hilarity. The wistful smile can remain in place. Two years of suffering over an unforgivably bad review that never happened! All you had to do was read it.

### October 28, 2016

J.H. Prynne is the magus of incomprehensibility. No one does it with more conviction. Open a Prynne text at random and – it's there, the magic touch:

Never or, will to it, nerve throw past most
over soon after, and grasp again offensive
likely before ever mud downwards cut, snip
relative to next time beset play genuine it
break

Since *Force of Circumstance* (1962), his first book, Prynne has inscribed secret codes, seldom flirting with communication. He takes English words and arranges them in a syntax of which only he and a few devotees know the purpose:

By the or and or other near true, yet as done
to allow this for also, for the for than
over far found extravagant inlet

Or we thought he knew. From an interview in the Fall issue of the *Paris Review*, we learn that even Prynne, the Life Fellow of Gonville and Caius College, Cambridge, has scant idea of what Prynne the poet is getting at. His *Paris Review* interviewers cunningly ask him to comment on a passage of his own work, which one reads aloud: 'For sure not in good likeness, profile in slant along the catchment / proposed, the speech corridor', etc. The recital over, Prynne is nonplussed. 'Well, I wouldn't like to be confronted with a passage like that, now that we've propounded it. I'd walk out, I think.'

In 2011, Prynne had 'one of those feelings that I sometimes have, that maybe I'm about to write something'. He checked into a hotel in Thailand, carrying one book in his luggage: V. Adrian Parsegian's *Van der Waals Forces: A Handbook for biologists, chemists, engineers and physicists*. He began to write a poem. 'I had no idea what its subject matter was going to be. I had no idea about its range of material. I had no idea about its prosodic formulism.' After four or five hours of 'feverish' writing, he would break off, perhaps to read *Van der Waals Forces*, before continuing:

'By the time I got to page twenty-plus, I had no idea what the rest of it was about, because I'd never once turned the pages back to see what the earlier writing had been doing... Some of the things I wrote down aston-

ished me. I'd think, Did I write that? Don't ask! Did I mean that? Don't ask!'

The interview is also of interest for revealing Prynne's political standpoint, a brand of old-school Maoism:

The narrative that Mao Zedong invented and devised to produce a native Chinese style of Marxism was and is still extremely interesting to me... It's still an active part of my thinking practice, which is curious because it's no longer part of the intellectual world of the Chinese... I would have been more comfortable in the bad period of Chinese Maoism than I am in the good period of post-Maoist China.

Politics have informed the poetry. Discussing his own book *Down where changed* (1979), Prynne states that it is one of several to have conducted a 'part argument against clemency. The argument is that mercy is a serious disruption of the moral order . . . and that means that mercy is an extravagant extra.' When next confronted by an inscrutable Prynne poem, and hearing yourself mutter, 'Have mercy, old boy', understand that there is none.

### August 2, 2019

Is it ok? Not everything is these days. Joe Cain, Professor of History and Philosophy of Biology at University College London, has decided it is not ok for a lecture theatre at his university to be named after Francis Galton (1822–1911). Galton's name is 'linked with racist, misogynist and hierarchical ideologies', and virtuous Professor Cain refuses to teach there.

Is it ok to read Vladimir Nabokov? The retiring editor in chief at Jonathan Cape, Dan Franklin, has said that he would not publish *Lolita* now. Is it ok to admire T.S. Eliot? ('My house is a decayed house, / And the Jew squats on the window sill', among other unprintables.) Ezra Pound? How could you, after reading his view that 'Adolf' was 'clear on the bacillus of kikism'? Is it ok to read Philip Larkin, racist and pornographer? William Faulkner? Oh boy. The phrase 'trigger warning' might have been coined to protect the young against the traumas that lie in store for a reader of *Absalom, Absalom!* Is it ok to read William Burroughs, merciless pursuer of boys in Tangiers? What about Chester Himes, the fourth corner of the Ralph Ellison–Richard Wright–James Baldwin quadrangle? An article in the *LRB* last year offered more detail than you needed to know about how he beat black and white women black and blue.

It is not ok to like Norman Mailer. Don't even ask about Henry Miller. The question of whether it's ok to read John Updike was addressed in the *TLS* recently by Claire Lowdon (it is) who, in the course of the article, also cast forgiving glances in the direction of Bellow, Roth and other big male beasts.

The beast is not exclusive to America. It is really not ok to read Guy de Maupassant. If you think it is ok to adore Flaubert, you haven't opened his letters from Egypt. Is it ok to read Albert Camus, that modern saint? You know the one, whose adultery drove his wife to attempt suicide. How can it be ok to read Louis Althusser, wife strangler? It is so not ok to read Kipling's 'If' that it was removed from a wall at Manchester University to protect students. It has been replaced by some deeply ok and deeply awful lines by Maya Angelou.

Perhaps it's better not to read at all, which is what lots of people are doing anyway. Some say we should be debating these matters. If we organize a talk on the subject, will you take part? The venue is the Galton Lecture Theatre, University College London.

### September 6, 2019

With even a minimal interest in modern poetry, you should be able to formulate answers to the following: 'What, in your view, have been the most (a) encouraging, (b) discouraging features of the poetry scene during the past decade?'

The commonest responses to both parts of the question will inevitably gesture towards diversity. There are more women poets, more BAME, more LGBT, all encouraging. North of the border, someone will be discouraged by the continuing neglect of MacCaig, Morgan, Crichton Smith, Mackay Brown. Will anybody respond to (a) with news of an interesting new school, or the emergence of 'a really big talent' that makes 'the business of reading poetry exciting once more'? Who sets the scene for appreciation of poetry today anyway? What *is* the scene? Hollie McNish or A.E. Stallings?

The words about an exciting 'big talent' are those of Philip Larkin, made in the course of his response to questions (a) and (b) when asked in 1972. A symposium on 'The State of Poetry' was published in Ian Hamilton's little magazine *the Review* that year. Larkin said that the most encouraging features of the past decade (the 1960s, in effect) were the good poems. The most discouraging? The bad ones. You'd think the same answer would do today, but no one likes to say how bad the bad ones are, for fear of being accused of something awful.

*The Review* put the questions to thirty-five active writers, all but two of them men, all of them 'white' (a debatable category, but let's move on), none outspokenly gay. Thom Gunn either was not asked or did not reply. Edwin Morgan, though he had written many poems of love and loss, had yet to come out of the closet.

Several of those questioned expressed surprise at Hamilton's choice of words. 'Poetry 'scene', is it?' (Julian Symons) 'No doubt the salient development is the one (consciously?) signalled by your use of the phrase 'the poetry scene'.' (John Fuller) 'The 'poetry scene' is recognizably a phrase of our own time, and stands for something very discouraging indeed.' (Martin Dodsworth)

There would be no such fastidiousness now. What was the problem? The 'scene' was the Mersey Scene: Brian Patten, Adrian Henri, Roger McGough. David Harsent's feeling was typical: 'A nasty piece of cross-breeding between the Beats and rock music spawned a gruesome monster in Liverpool.' Clive James joined in. 'I can't get discouraged or even bored by the success of the Liverpudlians in particular or the artless unwashed in general.' One of the Liverpudlians, gamely invited to contribute, was Adrian Henri. He could not have seen James's response in advance, but had no need to. 'If I were Clive James, no doubt the answer to the question would be (a) me, (b) you!'

His reaction to the unwashed notwithstanding, James did not wish to take 'the Roy Fullerish mandarin disapproval – ramrod-backed on the last bastion, defending standards to the final yawn'. As chance would have it, Roy Fuller contributed too. Imagine coming on like this today: 'Like the increase of educational opportunity, in the field of poetry the increased ease of publication and of public appearance has been of dubious benefit.'

To read the symposium almost fifty years on is to ask oneself, over and again: Would they say the same things now? Alan Brownjohn disliked the Liverpudlians, but detested 'the poetry of modern "folk"... It is worse than the worst of Liverpool. Dylan thinks he's *good*'.

What a thought. Back numbers of *the Review*, if you come across them, are always worth picking up. If only for the opportunity to marvel at how much the poetry scene has changed.

# Five Poems

## JULIAN BRASINGTON

## Rewriting the Triads of the Island of Britain

*After the medieval Trioedd Ynys Prydein*

April, end of, blue sky, a chill in the air
one of the Fortunate Men of the Island of Prydein
sitting in a garden overlooking the sea
listening to blackbirds, the far-off shut of a door
I am rewriting the Triads, remembering
Rosa, Marie, Julia Long Golden Hair,
Three Women who Received the Beauty of Eve
and how like the sea they slipped from me
too easily – a litany of waves falls and
overwrites its moment.  O, how the sun silvers
the sea's hand in the evening, it draws me back
to the Three Great Enchantments
and my work, listing – Capital,
the Solace of Purchase, its Pleasant Green –
and though the blackbirds sing, the Three
Steeds of Burden, Three Horses of Plunder
lumber onto my tongue and I wonder
what is it about Britain that names surfeit
like floods in spring for the Three Arrogant Men,
the Three Men of Shame, the Three Hard Slaps
that fell on the Island of Prydein
in the Year of our Lord, 2021.

*The epithets in this poem are taken from Rachel
Bromwich's collation of* Trioedd Ynys Prydein /
the triads of the island of Britain.

## Bedd Taliesin

Not grave enough
this cist for one so versed in court,
but I would take it

without the need to visit again,
holding still its random pillars
in my mind's eye, its graze

rough capstone
table enough for glass or flask
and someone to say, I was here too.

*Bedd Taliesin looks out from the Cambrian
Mountains to the Dyfi estuary and is held in
folklore to be the grave of the sixth-century
Poet, Taliesin.*

## Memorial, St Baglan's Church, Llanfaglan

And also their fifth son
who gloriously fell while leading the forlorn
hope at the memorable siege of Badajoz

a fierce Welshman, preferring
the white-eyes of night battle
to these silent hills, the Menai's race.

What dreams take a man
to war's red tide, where a Viscount's gift
is death-bed promotion?

Sweeter perhaps than Mary Owen's eyes
the catch of a lychgate –
retrenchment, breach, cunette.

## Tales

What if I do not leave a mark
an act, a monument, a book
that someone would want to make
a book of me, a thing and say
he thought these thoughts
did these things, was not altogether
good – might I then escape
clean away, hold myself half true
until perhaps some passing trowel
should raise my bones upon a table
two thousand years hence and say
he was a man who lived on meat
and did not suffer wounds.

## Above Llanfairfechan

October, middle of, a slight chill in the air,
I'm sitting in the garden listening to a dog yelp
on the far hill, the year gathering its short clothes
for today's last hurrah.  Tomorrow, I hear,
in the butcher's, the plastic-free shop, on the street
it will turn cold, and doom lies heavy upon us,
so I let the sun play on me soft fireside warmth,
watch the last breeze of summer drag its heels
through the oak leaves, the Menai slowly empty
and in its way, were this all it would be perfect
but for the ins, the outs, of a left-behind wasp
wondering – here
here
no, there.

# Kafka and the Body

## DAVID HERMAN

*Franz Kafka: The Drawings*, **edited by Andreas Kilcher (Yale University Press) £40.00 HB**

'His writing is more physical, more bodily and quivering than that of any other writer,' Gabriel Josipovici wrote of Kafka in *The Mirror of Criticism* (1983). It's not just that Kafka writes so powerfully about bodies. It's the extraordinary range of things that happen to bodies in Kafka's writing. The traditional boundaries between humans and animals or between objects and people collapse. Impulsive or convulsive bodies are always threatening to break out of control in a world of order, control and repression. Above all, bodies are subjected to extraordinary violence from *Metamorphosis* to *In the Penal Colony.*

The publication of a new book, *Franz Kafka: The Drawings*, raises a number of important questions, but perhaps the most interesting concerns the relationship between the way Kafka wrote about suffering bodies and how he drew them.

Until recently only a few of Kafka's drawings were widely known, primarily as illustrations on the covers of paperback editions of works published since the 1950s. Then in 2019 hundreds of drawings by Kafka (1883–1924), which had for years been locked away, became available following an extraordinary ten-year-long trial in Jerusalem which entrusted Kafka's papers that were previously in private hands to the National Library of Israel (see Benjamin Balint's fascinating book, *Kafka's Last Trial*, 2018).

*Franz Kafka: The Drawings* is the first book to publish all of Franz Kafka's available drawings, almost 250, including the newly discovered sketches. '[T]his collection of papers,' writes the editor, 'represents the last great unknown trove of Kafka's works.' In addition, there are a number of essays by leading critics and Kafka specialists, including Judith Butler and Andreas Kilcher. The drawings and essays in *Franz Kafka: The Drawings* will open up new ways of thinking about Kafka's drawings, of course, but also about his writing.

Kafka's drawings, writes Kilcher in his Introduction, cover his whole career, but he drew most intensively in his university years when he was studying in Prague in the early 1900s. It was during this time that he met his lifelong friend, later his literary executor, Max Brod (1884–1968), who collected and preserved these drawings. Kafka, Brod wrote in 1948, 'was even more indifferent, or perhaps better, more hostile to his drawings than he was to his literary production. Anything that I didn't rescue was destroyed.... I rescued them from the waste basket – indeed, I cut a number of them from the margins of the course notes from his legal studies.' In his will and testament, Kafka famously requested that both his drawings and his writings be destroyed ('please burn every bit of it without reading it, and do the same with any writings or drawings that you have, or that you can obtain from others').

The complicated history of Kafka's drawings, how they ended up with Brod, who took them to safety in Tel Aviv, how Brod gave his entire estate and papers to Ilse (later Esther) Hoffe, whom he met in 1942, and who 'was and is' much 'more' than just 'my secretary', is clearly told by Andreas Kilcher in his Introduction, though it is curious that he doesn't refer more to Balint's recent book.

The drawings, presented chronologically, consist of three groups. First, those from his university years. These are not connected to any texts. The second, much smaller group, includes drawings created in the context of letters, diaries and notebooks between 1909 and Kafka's death in 1924. The third group 'consists of ornamental figures that have their origins in the writing process.'

The most interesting drawings are figurative works. 'Kafka's drawings,' writes Kilcher in his essay, 'Kafka's Drawing and Writing', 'generally suggest human faces and figures with only a few strokes. The expressions and postures are not static, but often dynamic, sometimes leaning as if in motion... Particularly typical subjects of these drawings include fencers, horseback riders, and dancers.' (p.253) Kilcher quotes from Janouch's *Conversations with Kafka* (first published in Czech in 1947): 'We [Jews] cannot depict things statically. We see them *always in transition, in movement, as change* [my emphasis].'

The opposition between movement and immobility, confinement and breaking free, is one of the great themes in Kafka's writing. 'Motionless' is one of the key words in *Metamorphosis*: Gregor 'sat there motionless', his mother 'found him gazing out of the window, quite motionless', he lay 'motionless on the sofa', 'he would lie motionless for hours'. But words like 'motionless', 'immobile' and 'without motion' recur through much of Kafka's greatest writing.

This makes the eruption of movement in his fiction all the more striking. *Metamorphosis* ends as his sister 'sprang to her feet first and stretched her young body'. *The Judgment* ends as Georg 'rushed down' the staircase, 'rushed' out of the front door, 'swung himself over' the railings and 'let himself drop'. The drawings capture exactly the same contrast between movement and immobility.

There is something else which is striking about the drawings. 'The sketches,' Kilcher continues, 'are minimalistic from the standpoint of draftmanship, often reduced to a few symbolic lines and strokes, with an effect that is frequently fragmentary, tentative, unfinished.' (p.253) 'Most of them [his subjects] are not fully elaborated bodies or portraits,' writes Kilcher. 'They are not fleshed out and situated in three-dimensional space, they do not have fully developed physiques. On the contrary, they are generally free-floating, lacking any surroundings, and in themselves they are disproportional, flat, fragile, caricatured, grotesque, carnivalesque... In general, the most prominent features of these figures are extremities, such as legs, arms, and noses.' (p.253–4)

This is similar to a sentence in Gabriel Josipovici's essay *Kafka's Children* (republished in his book, *The Singer on the Shore*, 2006). He writes of the world of Kafka's 'febrile drawings', 'which show ludicrously tall or squat people stretching, twisting, leaning towards or away from one another in what would be grotesque if it was at attempt at realism, but which instead conveys perfectly how we sometimes feel constrained in our bodies and lunging free, both playing a game and close to desperation.' But there is something else to these ludicrous and grotesque figures. These figures also remind us of a passage from Kafka's story *Description of a Struggle*: 'Last night, Annie, after the party, you remember, I was with a man the like of whom you've certainly never seen. He looked – how can I describe him to you? – like a stick dangling in the air...'

What is striking about these figures, as with so many of his literary characters, is their lack of interiority and distinctive features. There's a fascinating blankness about them, which Kilcher at one point rightly compares to Paul Klee. 'He has no interest in psychology,' wrote Zadie Smith almost twenty years ago, 'not as something that individuates our tastes, desires, needs, opinions.'

It's true that Kafka's characters have plenty of what seem to be feelings. Joseph K in *The Trial* is 'angry', he reacts 'in amazement', 'in astonishment', 'had sunk again into vacant melancholy', 'bewildered', in a 'state of agitation', 'absent-minded'. But that's not the same thing as having an inner life. Kafka's characters speak (albeit strangely, even convulsively), things happen to them, but they don't really have selves or inner lives. It's because the stories are about something else: violence, being trapped or immobile, unable to escape and when they do escape it often has fatal consequences. His characters have bodies, but somehow these bodies are uninhabited. His figures are the same. They don't smile or frown or show any kind of feelings. They are bodies not people, unless, of course, this is how you think people are.

The book, Kilcher's essay in particular, are full of fascinating insights into the artistic world of early twentieth-century Prague and Kafka's interest in modern art. Kilcher traces Kafka's interest in art back to his days at school and especially at university, where he attended lectures in art history as well as in law, German literature and philosophy. Even after graduating, writes Kilcher, 'Kafka remained intensely engaged with art in a variety of ways', visiting exhibitions and museums in Prague but also when he travelled abroad, reading books by artists from van Gogh's letters and Gauguin's autobiography to books by Rodin and forming friendships with young artists. This is fascinating but doesn't help make sense of these strange figures in his own drawings. Visiting the Louvre or attending lectures in art history may reveal an interest in art, but it doesn't explain why Kafka drew these kinds of figures.

The lack of features or particularity gives the figures a kind of universality. But there is also another way of reading this. The Jewishness of Kafka's social circle and the antisemitism of early twentieth-century Prague, and central Europe more widely, are not properly addressed in these essays, and there is little attempt to put the drawings in the historical context of antisemitic violence in central Europe.

In *Kafka's Last Trial*, Balint quotes this passage from Kafka, from a letter written to his sister Elli in the last months of his life:

'Recently I had an amorous escapade. I was sitting in the sun in the Botanical Gardens... when the children from a girls' school walked by. One of the girls was a lovely long-legged blonde, boyish, who gave me a coquettish smile, turning up the corners of her little mouth and calling out something to me. Naturally I smiled back at her in an overly friendly manner, and continued to do so when she and her girlfriends kept turning back in my direction. Until I began to realize what she had actually said to me: "Jew".'

This twist at the end brings us to Kafka's stick-figures. Their lack of features means many things, but one thing it means is that the figures are not Jewish. It is easy to overlook this, but when we are talking about the antisemitic world of early 1920s Prague we shouldn't miss its importance. Two years before, Germany's Jewish foreign minister Walther Rathenau was assassinated by right-wing extremists. Kafka remarked that it was 'incomprehensible that they should have let him live as long as that'. That same year, in 1922, Kafka watched students of the German University in Prague riot rather than receive their diplomas from a Jewish rector.

The book concludes with several essays. The first, also by Kilcher, puts Kafka's drawings in their biographical and historical context; the second is a more general essay by the critic Judith Butler on the artistic treatment of the human body and on Kafka's works as a whole; the third is a *catalogue raisonné* by Pavel Schmidt, including the title, date, medium, dimensions and first printing of each drawing.

Butler's essay is the only one that attempts to contrast Kafka's drawings with his writing. Both, she begins, engage the questions 'Is it possible to touch the ground? And does a sketch of the body vacate the very need for ground?' (p.277) In Kafka's writings, Butler argues, 'there seems to be a recurrent desire or propulsion to resolve embodied existence into a pure line, void of substance and weight, suspended in air, without gravity, empowered by the loss of its own volume.' (p.281)

In the drawings, however, 'the figures, 'vacating volume, weight, and gravity, seem to minimize the body in an anorexic trajectory... Becoming line is becoming lean, but also becoming impossibly light, leaving the ground,' (p.289) as the body in Kafka's drawings seeks its dissolution 'into line, motion, and air, a fugitive figure, eluding capture.' (p.291)

Except when it doesn't, of course. There is nothing 'impossibly light' about Gregor Samsa or the man trapped in the lethal machine in Kafka's masterpiece, *In the Penal Colony*. The first time we encounter the prisoner, we read of the soldier 'who held the heavy chain controlling the small chains locked on the prisoner's ankles, wrists, and neck...' Or think of Gregor Samsa 'curtaining and confining of himself' in *Metamorphosis*, the ape 'inside a cage' in *Report to an Academy* or the Hunger Artist in 'his small barred cage'. Or 'those constraining corridors and boiler-rooms', in *Amerika*, what Josipovici calls 'the space where Kafka's narrative can function'. On 21 October 1921, Kafka wrote 'the truth that lies closest, however is only this, that you are beating your head against the wall of a windowless and doorless cell'. Confinement and immobility are at the heart of much of Kafka's greatest writing. The impossibility of movement is not 'eluding capture'.

Some of the figures in Kafka's drawings could not be more different. Free-floating in space, sometimes in the margins of scraps of paper, postcards, diaries and notebooks, impossibly thin, isolated. But others, drawn in black ink, look trapped, fenced in by bars or railings, immobile on a chair or at a desk or captured on a small piece of paper, cut out of a sketchbook. These drawings from Kafka's university years in Prague are the most haunting, and it's not surprising that they were selected as covers by S. Fischer Verlag in the 1950s and early '60s for some of Kafka's greatest masterpieces, *The Trial*, *Amerika* and *The Judgment*.

Perhaps that is why the story of Kafka's manuscripts and drawings has come to fascinate us so much. Smuggled out of Prague in March 1939 by Max Brod in 'a bulky, cracked-leather suitcase stuffed with loose bundles' (Balint), on the last train to cross the Czech-Polish border before the Nazis closed it, then locked up in bank vaults in Zurich and Israel and only now, at last, liberated after a long trial. Escape and confinement are at the heart of the story of these drawings and they are at the heart of Kafka's fiction and some of his greatest drawings. *Franz Kafka: The Drawings* offers a fascinating introduction to his drawings, his interest in art and how he saw people. Perhaps most interesting of all, the way he drew people turns out to be uncannily similar to the way he wrote about them.

# Poems

## MARIA KROUPNIK

### translated from the Russian by Matilda Hicklin

\*\*\*

Why has my land borne such a burden?
Why has my land brought all this shame?
To lose children, to howl for mothers in pain,
gulping down dust, trampling time into the dirt.
Fate, the future, scattered like sand.
What should I do? What's in my hands?
They're empty. Through my fingers
slipped reality, like grains of wheat. Can't hold on.
To love? Settle down? Become a mum?
Look for work? Drop everything and run?
Where to? Questions without a voice or answer.
A newsfeed flashes before my eyes.
Despair and grief. There's no Saviour
and with tears of blood the Mother of God
will wash everything not made by us,
and we have to answer for it all.
My soul, why are you sleeping? Arise and hearken.
Reject the evil poison of the world.
Mourn the dead, help the living.
Love those who can be loved.
Love those who want to be different.
We will hereby prevail when we are defeated.
10.03.22

\*\*\*

– mmmmmmmm
– give me a quint

– a ticket
– a bit
of support
or a spot of opera
they're coming
– shower down flour
– we will sing our music

bright blue the sky,
sun up on high…
my little friend
is going south
or west
for the east is damned
excommunicated
forever marked
until this century's over
until the end of time

\*\*\*

'Let this victim to Baal be sent,
To the lions the martyr be thrown!
Thy God shall teach thee to repent!
From th' abyss he'll give ear to my moan.'

\*\*\*

de profundis,
my friend, dis-
cordance - the dominant component
of space and time
of our tribe's
tremolo,
voice is cracking,
wheezing
turns out covid
wasn't that bad
stayed at home
'repaired' the Primus
where there was a minus
before, now is
hypertonia,
systolic and fibrillation
needed urgent hospitalisation
acute manic psychosis
imperialistic gibberish
hallucinatory
ghosts of magnificence
spot the difference
distinctions
impede death
she doesn't care who she consumes
everyone who exists
who's still alive
will be devoured
she won't shed
a tear

        04.03.22

***

God... Forgive me...
– Stay at home!
– Mum, I don't want to argue with you.
I love you. Don't worry about me.
I'll explain everything to you later.
Wrap up warm. Get some fresh air.
Go for walks, call my brother for anything.
It does the heart good to be working.
Wear a mask. Don't watch TV.
Read books and hold steady.

***

The boys write home:
'Mum, they're making me sign something.
They won't say where they're taking me.
Mum, I love you.
I hope they don't kill me.'

***

News. Instagram. Kharkov chat:
'My routine on the second day is like so –

in the metro at night, in the morning run home,
before the shooting starts, brush my teeth,
make a hot lunch and have something to eat.
There's no fuel. Queuing in the streets.
We took turns to sleep again. It's terrifying.
The hourly siren wail is harrowing."

***

An air-raid... alarm... No.
Airless. Sickness.
The future is dissolved in crisis,
like water, an acid or alkali.
Lend a helping hand and provide
for the dead, the injured, the prisoners
civilians and soldiers.
Stop the carnage!
No more war!
Today everyone is in pain,
you and me, but not the same.
        26.02.22

*Maryushka the Firebird, or a backwards fairy tale*

there is no room no space
quiet empty in this place
no dogs no crickets
only mines two shreds
only a corpse under sand
only a red-taloned
raven flies overhead
swerves like a broken fence
windows with bullet holes
a body like a sack of coals
hands tied with a kerchief
pure white like bindweed
these were the rules of war
Marina is no more
bare feet in the sand
braids stretch to the riverbank

***

take me river
come on carry me dear
to another place to the waterfall
to any god at all
let him hear my words
let him battle the inferno
the stranger's evil eye
and the blind philistine
and the beast and the thief
so that he can't get to his feet
so that he can't sleep
so that his soul can't receive
any cover or closure
in the light all guilt is exposed

\*\*\*

hush Maryushka don't cry
in the yard the executioner strides
to the base of the barrel he'll scrape
everything he wants to he'll take
a jealous glance
greedy hands
an empty skull
that old makitra bowl
hide in the basement
so you won't get taken

\*\*\*

like Maryushka with clouds in her glance
like Maryushka with wreaths in her hands
a grey garland for the foe
a white garland just like snow
choose one quickly
it'll be your destiny
*20.03–6.04.22*

# Four Poems

## HSIEN MIN TOH

### First sight of Afghanistan

The Tajik soldier waved us on our way
with an admonition not to cross the river
delivered with a smile I hadn't expected,
and then there it was, right in front of us:
Afghanistan. Its hillsides sloped down
to the Panj, threaded with green along
indented watercourses shielded by rock.
Giant shrubs shaded the bank, magpies
flew over foam and, as the 4WD led us
from the temptation of a fordable river,
the Afghan stone edged into sullen grey
filed down to a single angle of descent
and continued rising into white snowcap.
You remained resolutely silent, even as
I saw you marvel at the valley unrolling
like woven patterns on a carpet before us.
But grandeur dulls through exposure, so
I had to ask Ernis about the seeming calm.
"The army is always watching," he said,
not even pausing as he curved the 4WD
along a ledge with a hundred-foot drop.
And there my curiosity might have been
cut short, except that he went on to say
that to get to Kabul the Wakhani Afghans
cross into Tajikistan. "Forget the war,"
he said. "For us, it's just another border."
At that point I offered you a dried apricot,
and you took it, returning me a crease
of a smile. That was enough to trade on.
Our border reopened. My curiosity faded.

### Throwing stones into Afghanistan

Our driver Ernis proved the best at it:
he selected flat stones of a certain heft
and sent them with a practised whip
at an angle into the wind to pick up lift.
Watching his stones trace a graceful arc
against a backdrop blue until gravity
brought them down into an explosion
of river gave us more pleasure than our
falling short. One time his stone sailed
perfectly eighty yards over the water
and crashed with a clack and scrabble
into loose gravel. "Don't hit any Afghans,"
I laughed. "Or they might shoot back."
Of course nobody was there, or nobody
we could see; grey slopes charged down
on stone waters with military discipline.
As it turned out, we wouldn't see a village
on the other side until we reached Nijgar,
but by Namadgut we couldn't point out
any difference between the serried fields
lined by low stone and irrigation channels
on either side, except for electrical wiring
lacing the right bank. "If folks back home
see this..." I exhaled, fingering my fraying
camera strap. "Here different from south,"
Ernis said. "Here they are all Wakhanis."
The next time we stopped at a riverbank,
I found a flattish stone, but I didn't try
hitting the other side. I sank that stone
into the Panj; whether to dam the flow,
build a bridge or send a token churning
countless miles downriver, who could say?

## North of Khorog

North of Khorog, we began our descent.
It grew warmer, but that could have been
sun mounting cloudless sky.  The road
traced the contours of scrubby rock, but
the Panj gave the clearest indications
as it shed its smooth salamander skin,
raised shimmering scales and began
pummelling the boulders in its way.
We watched the river rampaging from
its highland origins, as though dragging
its kin away from mountain tranquillity.
But whether one traces back to an origin
or is impelled by it, the curse of the self
is to be, definitively, a self. I shared this.
You frowned. "Sometimes other people
make monsters of us all. You only need
look to your left," you said but convinced
no one gesturing at a stumble of moraine.
Instead of replying, I watched the river
overflow submerged obstacles, creating
crests that crashed back on themselves.
It seemed that the Panj would never end.
We took a blind corner. Then the next.

## Last Sight of Afghanistan

The next day could scarcely have been
more different. A dozen miles west of
Kalai Khum, the road abruptly morphed
into tarmac. It felt as if we were flying,
even as the Panj did the exact opposite:
pushing through a broad basin where it
reflected pale hills into a narrow channel
where the waters jostled for right of way.
We passed several trios of Tajik soldiers
patrolling the road, lime green uniforms
not so much camouflage as a blazon
against these slopes of arid stone and
tired shrub, their AK47s tightly slung,
and then a blue sign for Ir Afghanistan,
set off from a red suspension bridge.
I took the wheel, bridged dry tributaries,
eased past a herd of slow loping cattle
and slid by an Opel needing a mechanic.
The automatic transmission switched
down a gear. The last I saw of the Panj
was a slow sliver of grey low to my left
as I took a right bend at twenty mph.
I think it was the Panj, but didn't stop
to confirm it. The slopes put on a coat
of green and copper. The flycatchers
darting past my windscreen were blue.

# Pioneers: The Iowa Writers' Workshop in the Early Fifties

## TONY ROBERTS

'We were pioneers, but did not know it', wrote author James B. Hall of the Iowa Writers' Workshop in the early fifties. It offered graduate fiction and poetry writing classes and its visiting faculty included John Berryman, Robert Lowell and Karl Shapiro, with appearances by Randall Jarrell, Dylan Thomas, John Crowe Ransom, Robert Penn Warren, Allen Tate and John Ciardi. These poets–several still building reputations in their late thirties – had in their classes some of the finest of the next generation of poet-teachers: Donald Justice, W. D. Snodgrass, Philip Levine, William Stafford, Jane Cooper, Robert Dana, Henri Coulette, William Dickey and others. The memories of that time and place of this younger generation, entertaining in themselves, are also illustrative of the nature of creative influence.

The founding director of the writers' programme had been Wilbur Schramm, but its fame resulted from Paul Engle's tireless efforts between 1941 and 1965. A native of Iowa and an alumnus of the university, Engle explained that it took imagination on the part of the university to invest in creative writing. After all, this was the first postgraduate writing degree on offer in America. In fact according to poet Robert Dana, an M.A. student there, 'in the 1950s, the writing program played no great role at the university. Kept on a short leash by a skeptical administration, it had at most only two or three assistantships to offer. It was a lean operation in lean times.' Warren Carrier, who taught there at the time, pointed to conflicts between the 'scholarly' members of the department and themselves.

Engle, however, proved adept at defending his territory. In his absences – often in pursuit of sponsors for the programme – he brought in rising names in the poetry world to take his place in teaching the appreciation and craft of writing. To Dana, 'He was sometimes the shrewd and hardheaded horsetrader he claimed his forebears had been. But he was also the scholar of literature who had won a Rhodes [scholarship] and crewed for Oxford, and who, at twenty-six, had been a poet of promise and of some achievement.'

Dana, later editor of *The North American Review*, also conceded that Engle could be 'enigmatic and contradictory and hard', a point W.D. Snodgrass took up elsewhere. He credited Engle's excellence as an administrator and acknowledged that he could be a brilliant teacher: 'I remember him introducing us to Baudelaire, Verlaine and Rimbaud, and making us see ways of meaning we'd never even thought of.' Snodgrass was, however, critical of Engle's poetry while, more importantly, he felt the director manipulated his students at times (cancelling grants – Snodgrass had been a casualty – and requiring menial tasks to be performed for him).

Against the uncertain background of the Cold War, aspiring and generally impoverished young writers, many with a service background, came to sit, learn and suffer (some offered a parallel with time spent on Devil's Island), in corrugated steel sheds, old barracks by the Iowa River. Robert Lowell later characterized the experience – on the dust-jacket of Snodgrass's stunning debut collection, *Heart's Needle* (1959) – as flowering in 'the most sterile of sterile places, a post war, cold war Mid-western university's poetry workshop for graduate students.'

Iowa City itself was not reckoned to be the most exciting of places. On his first visit, Lowell described it to Elizabeth Bishop as 'gray-white, monotonous, friendly, spread-out, rather empty, rather reassuring'. To his wife, Elizabeth Hardwick, it seemed 'a strange place... it's so flat and ugly and somehow has the air and look of a temporary town. Actually, anything over fifty years old is a landmark.' Its cultural capital appeared to be in foreign movies and New Criticism. James B. Hall would remember it as more colourfully exasperating: 'Life in Iowa City was at once terribly high minded, demanding, and – always – no end in sight. Each spring there was a sensational murder of some kind; the divorce rate was too high to be exemplary. The period vice was drink, with no upper level stated on consumption, either.'

At the time Engle summoned them, Berryman, Lowell and Shapiro had been given a lot of attention from the literary world. Shapiro and Lowell had each won a Pulitzer Prize: for *V-Letter and Other Poems* in 1945 and *Lord Weary's Castle* in 1947. Berryman stood between *The Dispossessed* 1948 and 'Homage to Mistress Bradstreet', which appeared in *Partisan Review* in the fall of 1953, the year his first marriage effectively ended. When he took over from Lowell for the first of two semesters at Iowa, in spring 1954, his mental and physical health were suffering.

Randall Jarrell appeared first. He had been invited to give a reading of poems and discuss students' work in April 1952 and wrote, thrilled, 'Well, I've had a wonderful time here at the University of Iowa! I never saw such a pleasant, unspiteful, un-nasty-intellectual bunch of poets as here.' He mentioned Justice and Snodgrass. 'I talked to them and some others about 2 ½ hours yesterday afternoon about their poems and poetry. Last night I read... I've never in my whole life been so successful with an audience; by the time I was 2/3 through, there was such rapport that we were like mother and long-lost child... I've never, almost, felt more strongly what a wonderful thing it is to have made the poems and have moved people so.'

Iowa proved no such epiphany for Lowell and Berryman. There would be much discussion among the participants of the classes over the years as to the teaching of each. Lowell came first to the workshop in 1950 and taught there again in 1953. His first stint seems to have been the quieter. He had married Hardwick in July 1949, then been hospitalized until that December for what would be eventually diagnosed as bipolar disorder. At the prospect of teaching, he wrote to his college friend, the novelist Peter Taylor, that he might meet 'frightfully brilliant' students and so he was preparing as if for a PhD examination. Part of the fear, of course, had been Lowell's inexperience as a teacher, part his recent health and part, perhaps, teaching veterans on the G.I. Bill.

The class of twenty-five aspiring poets turned out to be much friendlier ('There are no fireworks,' he reported). To Bishop he elaborated: 'O, and the poems! Everything from poetry society sonnets to the impenetrably dark – defended with passion, shyness, references to Kant and Empson mysticism. About six of my students are pretty good – at least, they do various things I can't and might become almost anything or nothing.'

Emboldened, the Lowells returned to Iowa in spring 1953. This time he had twenty-three students in their twenties, a workshop and courses in French poetry and Homer in the original Greek to teach (with classicist Gerald Else). Lowell did not make a great deal of the visit, writing to Allen Tate that he had good students, some confused and, like a psychiatrist, had offered 'banal worldly wisdom'. By the beginning of 1954, he admitted to Bishop, they were 'sick of Iowa City' and were moving on to a teaching appointment in Cincinnati. After his mother's death early in the year, he would suffer another manic episode.

The students anticipated Lowell's arrival as a major event. He was, after all, something of firebrand by poetic reputation. Among those waiting was Donald Justice, already well-travelled in the academic and poetry worlds. He knew Frost through Frost's grandson, Lowell and Jarrell through their college classmate, the author Peter Taylor (his wife's sister's husband). Having grown up in Florida, Justice had earned degrees at the University of Miami and North California, before studying at Stanford, where he came under the influence of Yvor Winters. He had published a little, also.

Justice had arrived at Iowa at the suggestion of Taylor and Robie Macauley, taking up an assistantship to teach fiction writing. He would go on to teach at the writers' workshop for many years and win awards for his thirteen collections of poetry, from a Lamont Poetry Prize for his first collection, *The Summer Anniversaries* (1960) to a Pulitzer Prize for his *Selected Poems* (1979), and a Bollingen Prize in 1991.

Unlike the Lowells, Justice found the life of the town exciting. He remained equally positive about the classroom: 'I thought Lowell was an excellent teacher. He was someone of great intensity, to whom everything mattered. There was a distance, a decent and probably self-protective distance... As well, I liked him a lot personally, and he was always very kind to me. All the same, if I don't remember him quite the way Phil does, it's nevertheless true that Lowell was more interested in what he himself was writing than in what his students were doing... It's also true that there was a hint of condescension in his regard for student work.'

The 'Phil' he referred to was Philip Levine, a native of Detroit, who had had a tough working life from the age of fourteen. The opening of an early poem, 'On the Edge', is identifiably his:

My name is Edgar Poe and I was born
In 1928 in Michigan.
Nobody gave a damn. The gruel I ate
Kept me alive, nothing kept me warm,
But I grew up, almost to five foot ten,
And nothing in the world can change my weight.

After earning his B.A. at Wayne University in 1950, Levine had worked hard shifts in the automobile industry, before marrying and attending (without registering) at Iowa. He would also teach there, finally settling at California State University, Fresno, and win, among other honours, a National Book Award for *Ashes: Poems New and Old* (1979) and a Pulitzer Prize for *The Simple Truth* (1994).

Like Snodgrass, Levine proved quite forthright about his teachers at Iowa: 'To say I was disappointed in Lowell as a teacher is an understatement', he wrote. He felt Lowell taught 'badly' (being competitive, playing favourites, misreading poems, imposing his own work on the class). He had – according to Levine – given the impression 'that there was a secret, a hidden key, to the reading of poetry', yet would never 'unlock the secret door to understanding' for his students. Instead, he stared at their incomprehension and rejected their efforts at explication of poems by Housman, Ransom and Pound. (Ironically, on 10 March, Lowell had written to his mother regarding what was required of a new teacher and had stressed, 'To know how a poem is put together and what it *means* – no amount of enthusiasm or energy can relieve you of that duty'.)

Levine had other charges to level: 'His fierce competitiveness was also not pleasant to behold: with the exceptions of Bishop and Jarrell, he seemed to have little use for any practicing American poet, and he once labeled Roethke 'more of a woman than Marianne Moore'. He offered a further damaging suggestion, 'Lowell was, if anything, considerably worse in the seminar; we expected him to misread our poems – after all, most of them were confused and, with a very few exceptions, only partly realized, but to see him bumbling in the face of "real poetry" was discouraging.'

Most of his students, Levine reckoned, failed to attend throughout the semester, though he remained: 'I stayed to the bitter end, and felt exactly as Lowell wanted me to feel: honored to be in his company'. He then 'discovered that one-to-one Lowell could be both helpful and encouraging', directing him back to Hardy, 'for which I am still thankful'. Levine did make a further concession: 'In fairness he was teetering on the brink of a massive nervous breakdown... Rumours of his hospitalization drifted back to Iowa City, and many of us felt guilty for damning him as a total loss.'

Levine's seems to have been a minority view. Neither Dana nor Snodgrass accepted Levine's perspective on Lowell's teaching, though all acknowledged the fact that he did not encourage familiarity. Dana, who was to teach at Cornell for forty years, wrote, 'I recall neither his boredom nor overt acts of favoritism. If anything, Lowell permitted, whether from generosity or sloth, a wider range of what might be called "amateurism" than Berryman would allow later. In fact, Donald Petersen's description of Lowell's classroom manner seems to me entirely accurate... "he praised what he could in our poems and diffidently suggested that we consult other poets' works, to see how it was done this or that way. He seldom suggested any specific revisions."'

His impact seems to have been, for Dana, more subtle: 'It may have been partly Lowell's influence that caused Henri Coulette and others to enroll in courses in the classics department, and which caused me later to undertake a translation of Rilke's *Letters to a Young Poet*. He had a way, however indirectly, of pushing you.' Dana also felt Lowell's influence when he came to drop 'uniqueness of idiom as a literary value', as Lowell had in *Life Studies*.

Snodgrass, the poet whose early work most resembled (and influenced) Lowell's, came to Iowa after war service in the navy. He later taught at a number of universities, winning the 1960 Pulitzer Prize for *Heart's Needle.* Both Jarrell and Lowell mentioned him in their letters, the former describing him as 'inspired', the latter acknowledging that he had written a couple of the best poems by his students at Iowa and, 'I now think he is incomparably the best poet we've had since you started.'

He had come from Empson to Lowell, after Eliot's 'etiolated language and attitudes', and remembered the students as 'ravenous' for the 'vigour' of Lowell's poetry. In person he had proved, 'the gentlest of mortals, clumsily anxious to please'. Snodgrass went on to say, 'However high the expectations, almost no one was disappointed by Lowell's teaching – it was only years later, from comments published in *The Gettysburg Review*, that I learned of Philip Levine's resentment.'

Lowell's courses on masterpieces of English poetry continued to inspire him: 'For each session he picked a poet or even a single poem, then for several hours would free-associate to that work. Wyatt, Raleigh, Milton's "Lycidas", Landor, Tennyson's "Tithonus" – week after week we came away staggered under a bombardment of ideas, ideas, ideas.... Who could feel less than grateful for a mind so massive, so unpredictable, so concerned?'

Snodgrass's reminiscences of Randall Jarrell came from his time in Iowa and from a conference in Boulder, Colorado, which took place around the same time. As a teacher Jarrell delighted but surprised him: 'Slender and graceful, with a pencil-line moustache, he displayed the manners and vocabulary of a lively but spoiled little girl.' In contrasting their teaching styles, Snodgrass observed, 'Lowell's analyses had tended to the highly intellectual; Jarrell's, the emotional and personal'. He tended to discuss individual student's work in private, which did not always satisfy the class, though in these sessions he could be 'remarkably kind' about their poems. Snodgrass appreciated the fact that Jarrell helped change the direction of his work. 'Snodgrass, you're writing the very best second-rate Lowell in the whole country!' he once declared.

While there remains the difference of opinion on Lowell's teaching, there appears to have been general agreement on the startling effect John Berryman could have in class. His time in Iowa City did not begin auspiciously, however. After unpacking and drinking with old friends: 'Hall dark, steep stair down, travel blind, I crasht/& snapt a wrist, landing in glass'.

The broken wrist and swollen ankles incapacitated him for days, though he went on to dazzle his class with the greats in poetry and poems by his contemporaries (Lowell, Bishop and Roethke). Donald Justice reckoned he was the best of his teachers there: 'He was full of a kind of fervour or fire, in class and out. In class he was a master of detail and care; he was in love with the whole business of reading and writing and talking about it, in love with teaching itself, though he had not done much of it.' To Justice, while not a model, Berryman showed genuine interest in the work of his students.

Justice was also, memorably, the young poet who stunned Berryman in class with the quality of his sonnet 'The Wall', which begins:

The wall surrounding them they never saw;
The angels, often. Angels were as common
As birds or butterflies, but looked more human.
As long as the wings were furled, they felt no awe.

For this he received the astonished: 'It is simply not right that a person should get a poem like *that* as a classroom assignment.' The poem remains one of Justice's best and best-known. That year Berryman helped him toward an Iowa-Rockefeller grant in poetry ('I should place him very close to W.S. Merwin and Anthony Hecht, who seem to me the best American poets younger than Lowell'). He seems to have been most impressed by Justice of all the Iowa students, for his work and possibly for his reliability. In lieu of a will, he wrote instructions in 1959 naming Justice after Lowell as adviser on the publication of his 1947 sonnets. He recommended the younger poet's work to Dwight Macdonald – then a staff writer for *The New Yorker* – to Catharine Carver at *Partisan Review*, and he also offered to write to a senior editor at Scribner's on behalf of *The Summer Anniversaries*.

Jane Cooper, a poet who later taught at Sarah Lawrence College for forty years, remembered Berryman's speaking with 'great delicacy and warmth' of Roethke ('the only man who... *thinks* like a flower!'), though it was Philip Levine for whom Berryman was the greatest of teachers: 'He was the most brilliant, intense, articulate man I've ever met, at times even the kindest and most gentle, and for some reason he brought to our writing a depth of insight and care we did not know existed.'

Levine said that Berryman sensed and applauded the 'wonderful fellowship' among the students, burnishing it: 'These were among the darkest days of the Cold War, and yet John was able to convince us – merely because he believed it so deeply – that nothing could be more important for us, for the nation, for humankind, than our becoming the finest poets we could become.'

Two extraordinary high points, apparently, were Berryman's teaching of Whitman's 'Song of Myself' and Dylan Thomas's 'A Refusal to Mourn the Death, by Fire, of a Child in London'. Berryman loved Thomas as a friend and poet. To Levine, his performance remained unequalled ('Never again would I encounter so great a poem so perfectly presented'). There continued a friendliness and respect between the two.

On his part Snodgrass remembered, 'I could only get to an occasional class. As well as fighting to see my child, I was working as an aide in a hospital, so I didn't have much time left. But he *was* a very impressive teacher, and very different from anyone else I had had. I didn't always understand what he was saying. I couldn't work out what principles lay behind his judgments, couldn't even be sure that there were any such principles. But he was full of startling insights, and we learned a lot.'

Snodgrass credited his poem 'A Flat One' to Berryman's assignment on death, which prompted him to a subject he would not otherwise have tackled. This un-illusioned poem begins:

> Old Fritz, on this rotating bed
> For seven wasted months you lay
> Unfit to move, shrunken, gray,
> No good to yourself or anyone
> But to be babied – changed and bathed and fed.
> At long last, that's all done.

Berryman's commitment had its more disturbing edge. Apparently he reduced the oversubscribed class he had taken over from Lowell to thirteen students – removing what, to Levine at least, were hangers-on who were 'just horsing around' – by being particularly harsh about a poem by a doctor's wife. As Levine put it, 'In his workshop John was ruthless and screamingly funny: everyone… got leveled at one time or another.' He was given to sarcastic remarks: 'When I first saw your poems I thought you'd borrowed Cal's [Lowell's] old portable Smith-Corona'; 'If you're going to write something this long why don't you try making it poetry?' 'Yes, yes, you have a genuine lyrical gift, but who encouraged you to never make sense, always to be opaque?'

Biographer John Haffenden quotes another student of Berryman's as saying, 'And there was even more to learn from him outside of class as he talked almost exclusively about writing and writers & always in his tense, nervous, paranoid bombastic manner. Thinking back, I don't believe I've ever known a more gentle yet violent individual. In private, he was marvellously compassionate about his students and their work even though in class he was often devastatingly sarcastic, nasty and generally tough. But all of this was tempered by his brilliant wit and candid openness.'

In one letter Berryman described Philip Levine as 'a real tough guy & sensitive'. He had reason to know this from a drunken incident, which Levine did not repeat in his encomiums on his teacher, when he made a pass at Levine's girlfriend, hit him with a bottle and was punched as a result. The problem with Berryman, according to Snodgrass, was that 'as soon as he liked you he began making your life difficult by tampering in your love life and sometimes trying to tamper with your wife.' His total commitment to writing contrasted, according to another student, with 'his total desperation about himself, his relationships to others, and his compulsive daily self-assessment. And such awesome burdens of guilt about all aspects of his life!'

One incident illustrating Berryman's desperation involved his decision to take his own life, which was pre-

vented only by Donald Justice, who had been summoned by him. Seeing his professor with razor blades, Justice almost fainted, thereby becoming the patient. To balance the record Justice pointed out that Berryman's 'emotional peak' was not the only one at the time and also that he had a 'capacity for joy as well as suffering', and that there were calm and enjoyable tavern meetings. Eventually though, like Lowell, Berryman would write that he detested life in Iowa City. His miseries, he reported, included colitis, malnutrition, dyspnoea and insomnia.

Karl Shapiro, doubtless in better physical shape, had less of an impact in Iowa. He joined the faculty for a semester, commuting from Chicago one day a week. Justice found him less interesting as a teacher, though 'some of us were very fond of his new Adam and Eve sequence of poems, which had recently come out in *Poetry*'. He felt that perhaps Shapiro's sequence had influenced his own 'The Wall', but remembered only one remark from the classes, 'to the effect that we should never use anything literary as subject matter' – a remark occasioned, probably, by his proposed sonnet on Hamlet's father.

Snodgrass had less time for Shapiro ('oddly noncommittal, almost evasive'): 'Considering his position as editor of *Poetry* and the rambunctious heresy of his recent critical dicta, we were astonished at how vague he seemed about student poems.' Unsurprisingly, Snodgrass remembered Dylan Thomas at Iowa: 'We had the usual longed-for scandals: the stevedore's language, the crush on a dumpy local waitress, the Tournament of Insults at the chairman's party.' At a reading, 'Before and between poems, his speech was slurred, shambling, obscene; suddenly, for the poem, he would shift into that sonorous, nearly Shakespearean voice still so familiar on recordings. The effect was so electrifying that one couldn't help wonder how much it might be calculated.' At his meetings with the workshop, he passed over the students' poems, instead reading 'marvellously' his favourites'.

Snodgrass remembered also the New Critics, who made brief visits: Brooks, Tate, Warren, Ransom. He seems to have been underwhelmed by these Southern Agrarians, as 'dialect problems sometimes developed' and Warren, moreover, 'paced and mumbled'. He saved his strongest criticism for John Ciardi, translator of Dante, who 'brought a sense of emptiness and intellectual posturing', while 'his own poems, when he read them, seemed null or pretentious'.

In a depressing coda: John Berryman returned to Iowa for the fall term, only to be dismissed. This time he was to teach a course focusing on the idea of voice in the novel and a short story workshop with novelist Marguerite Young. A combination of heavy drinking and Young's approach led to Berryman's immediate disaffection. An argument erupted during only the second shared workshop, which caused Berryman to drink even more aggressively that night and led to his arrest for disorderly conduct. When the local paper picked up the story, he was dismissed. (Fortunately, his career was saved by Allen Tate, who found him a teaching post at Minnesota, where he remained.)

The Iowa Writers' Workshop boasts seventeen Pulitzer

Prizes, six recent Poet Laureates and dozens of other awarded to alumni over the eighty-six years of its existence. Its graduate writers' programme has become a place of myth as much as history, given that post-war record. As Paul Engle wrote with satisfaction of its poets in 1961, 'Their talent was inevitably shaped by the genes rattling in ancestral closets. We did give them a community in which to try out the quality of their gift.'

# Six Poems

### CATHERINE ESTHER-COWRIE

## Outside My Window

A dog. Her underbelly.
Fat hanging tits.
I think of the Dahomey Amazons.
Women who never knew a man,
never bore a child. Whose breasts
so stunned the Frenchmen. They couldn't shoot.
The Amazons severed their heads.
I have longed to suckle at their tits.
Mino. Mother. I would cry.
Each drop possessing what –
pride. Prophecy. A way forward.
My own legend:
A woman forced.
A woman forced. Who stayed.
Because sugar cane and cocoa failed.
Because a 1930s rural town.
He, a landowner.
Because, because, because
a song of shame fattens
on its own repetition,
I reach for another.
But what of Mino's song,
wild march to the battlefield,
her shame:
*We are men, not women.*
If I am the call: Mino. Mother.
What of her response:
I have no daughter.

## Reasons to Hit a Child

Because the sun grows in her left eye.

Because a misfired belt buckle.

Because her skin hasn't turned, and

Because the neighbors gossip that a white man
sleeps under your bed.

Because if you spare the rod, you spoil the child.

Because the porridge-sticky pan still sits on the
stove.

Because her mouth is so full of your name,
*Mama, Mama, Mama...*

Because as a child, you snapped branches in two,
kept time to a hand slapping your mother's face.

Because rage has its own flight.

Because there is a pleasure in pinching flesh
until it flashes red.

## Elegy

Here are the missing pigeon peas,
fallen to the ground
from the heart your son drew for you,
the heart he drew with a no. 2,
colored inside cerulean blue,
lined the edges with pigeon peas.

Here is the heart that falls out
from between the sheets of your master's thesis
stashed in the dust and webbed cupboard
of your father's house.

Uncle, I am seeing what you saw,
the lopsided writing, his name.
I am touching the hardened glue,
useless remanent.

We are throwing away your things:
*Mathematical Theory. Shane.*
The medical bills with their sharp
dollar signs.
A breeding ground for mosquitos,
we empty the cupboard.
You are seven years gone.
We throw the heart – your son I have never met.
Does he have your height?
Walk around with your Laurence Fishburn
look-a-like face?

I keep your copy of *Christian Sex*,
trace your underlining, the loud hum
of the body, your questioning
of waiting. I'm waiting. Poorly. Badly.

What gossip it was back then –
Your venture across the boundary,
the apathy of biology,
the tick, tick, ticking of your heart
in some far away land-locked country.

## Assimilation Disruptor

You struck the girl. She'd knifed the lizards
out of her tongue. Lizards you gave to her.
Then the mourning doves, hummingbirds, and a finch,
then the wind shushing through the stick-legged trees. Your song.
She was knifing out your song. You struck the girl.
Diseased her eyes. The skirting snow, she saw foam,
an ocean muscling its way across the suburbs,
overwhelming the pine and oak, her dreams –
She woke to the scent of nostalgia. Flicked on a light,
swore she saw it. From the corner of her left eye,
green hills, peaking.

## Rogue Memories, AKA The Beast

What shrieks cupboards until emptied,
falls down the backstairs scattering

into tiny, tiny pieces.
Has no face. Bares no teeth.

Chases the children here and there
with a flick, a lick, licks.

Only a small girl stays, puffy with hurt,
suckling the ear of her teddy bear.

Louds the clamor of thrown pots, choruses
the accompanying damn yous, through a window

hems a woman in. She is under the bed.
She won't come out, won't come out, she says.

Possesses no hands but conducts
the symphony of another's undoing

a sound. Slim, slender fingers undo

a sound, thread a ghost into the small,
small ear of a girl.

Amasses, legion, at the thin membrane
demanding tending. A witness.

Tears through anyway, a thousand
thousand little feet running through your head.

# Return for a Funeral: An Object Lesson

We press our fingers to their plastic shrines,
to their glass coffins,
visages captured in film.
What do we say now, how pretty,
how fat, how fair, how dark, too young
how badly the man she slept with treated her.
Divide the spoils, the silk,
the chiffon, the 100% cotton,
squabble over her gold hoops, bangles,
a nearly empty bottle of Casmaratti.
There are lessons here, the old women murmur,
beauty and charm vanish, they preach,
how living with a bad man killed you,
the stress raging the cells
until they collected, fisted into a lump.
I plastic-bag a purse and leather sling-backs,
O body of my sister, body I loved.
They expect me to talk about your sin,
how your friends only remember how
good you looked, copper-colored girl
who caught all the men.
As though sin is without hands,
your hands, slender,
copper-colored, holding mine.

# from *The Regulars*

## TUESDAY SHANNON

i.
His fist is as soft as a block
of butter, shaking
around two pound coins
and a twenty pence piece,
to be exchanged
for the first pint of the day.

Under the tap it pours
itself, clouds, settles
thick and brown with
a white halo the width
of forefinger and thumb.

His skin is the jaundiced shade
of pages in antique books,
and the ink of a decades-old tattoo
is blurred beyond comprehension

not that it matters
whether it reads Mother
or Martha, those who meant enough
to be honoured are long gone.

Nothing is left but this
small pleasure: the glass
sweating as the tremors still.

ii.
Dying midsummer light
softens the creases and lines on skin
as sheer as bible-paper, dims the pallor
of the thick blue rivers confluent
and divergent across each limb.

He can almost pretend
he doesn't notice that each breath
is laboured, or that despite cutting
her food into bite-sized chunks
she is eating less each day.

Each night the burden of lifting
her into bed is a little lighter,
a little heavier. Across the table
he clasps her hand, like a child
desperately holding his kite.

vi.
9:55, he paces as he waits for the bar
to be lifted from the heavy wooden door,
then filters in with the Thursday pension crowd.
After their orders of coffee, toast, seniors' breakfasts,
he asks for his drink in a tall glass, no ice –

and I am reminded of being fifteen,
refilling Dad's Smirnoff
to hide at the back of the cupboard.

His voice shows no trace of this town,
no drawn-out Midlands vowels, as he tells me
about a job interview in the city,
how he's having a few to settle his nerves.
The same lie he's told me seven times this year.

*Another one for the road.*

He hands back his glass and I pour again
because I am paid to oblige, nothing more.

He asks about me, and because I am paid to oblige
I tell him I'm working my way through university.

*My son did the same*, he replies,
though they've long been estranged.

*One more.* He smiles, I smile, and again I pour.
He downs in a gulp, then makes for the door.
*Good luck!* I call, but he's forgotten his lie.
He'll be back next Thursday, pension day, same time.

vii.
Outside, the church clock chimes eleven
and echoes through the empty marketplace –
the stalls' steel skeletons set up,
glowing white in the stark LED light,
awaiting the mornings' wares of knock-off
perfume and second-hand books.

When the bell rings for last orders
a small commotion ensues:
a rush for one more lager,
just another glass of wine.

The last pint poured and paid for,
I wipe down the bar, the tables, the menus,
collect the glasses brewing fag-ends,
make idle conversation with my captors:

*How's the kids?*
*How's work?*
*What's your mum up to these days?*

Then I fill every fridge,
unscrew each nozzle to soak overnight,
sweep, mop, cash up,
bar the door, turn out the lights.

# Hallowed Graves, Cold Remains

## J. KATES

'This sounds like Lowell translating Racine, making the clear things dark,' Richard Wilbur penciled in the margin of a poem he was critiquing, part of a manuscript I would be submitting for my Wesleyan degree in 1967.

So much packed into that one remark, not just the richly deserved critique of my own callow writing, a critique I have taken to heart ever since. It also speaks with the voice of Wilbur the Milton scholar ('dark with exceeding light') and the voice of Wilbur the literary rival of Robert Lowell, both as leading poets of their time and as translators. (They were born on the same day, although four years apart.)

An apprentice poet sorting out my own voices in the mid-1960s, I read Wilbur, a major figure on the Wesleyan campus, with some wonder and a great deal of appreciation; but I was far from being a follower, took no formal classes with him, and thought I was going my own way. Still, when his 'On the Marginal Way' appeared in *The New Yorker* in 1965, it struck me, as it still does today, in the heart. Reading that poem for the first time under the gloom of war-torn America, I danced in elation around my dormitory room to the craft and music of its hard-won affirmation in impossibly difficult times.

> Joy for a moment floods into the mind,
> Blurting that all things shall be brought
> To the full state and stature of their kind . . .

And at least one of my own poems of those years clearly is weighed down by Wilbur's direct influence – the fluid distance, the irregular tightly rhymed stanzas. I was awed when he agreed to be my thesis adviser, and I remained in awe of him all the rest of his life. He wrote me a generous note on the publication of my first chapbook, but I didn't have the courage to take that personally. He was generous with everyone.

I knew Lowell's poetry in the mid 1960s mostly from *For the Union Dead*, which came out in 1964. During that same war-torn gloom that 'On the Marginal Way' glowed through, Lowell took a more explicitly engaged stand than Wilbur did, and I read and admired him for his commitment more than for his literature. Lowell wrote of New England, which I was just coming to know in depth. His poems were to me inimitable in the sense that I had no literary desire to go where he was going. I had little sympathy then, and only slightly more now, for Lowell's (self-admitted) muddiness that Wilbur was using to critique my poem. Lowell has a lot to answer for as the father of flaccid autobiographical poetry and the abandonment of verse, but the best pieces in *For the Union Dead* stand up far better than I had remembered them, and I still place the title poem of that book on the same shelf as 'On the Marginal Way.'

Wilbur's translation of Molière's *Misanthrope* had appeared back-to-back with Lowell's *Phaedra* in 1961[3]. He went on to translate not only a whole corpus of Molière, but Corneille, too, while his own *Phaedra* was one of three Racine tragedies.

As I read Richard Wilbur's poetry today, I find it exquisitely *racinien*, both in subject and style. (Racine had been with me since high-school days of intensive French study.) He did not publish his own version of *Phaedra* until the 1980s, but during my time at Wesleyan I had gone through Wilbur's Molière line-by-line, side-by-side with the original French, marveling at the exactitude of correspondence as I was cutting my teeth on literary translation as a craft. *The Misanthrope* and *Tartuffe* underlined for me what was possible. Growing older as a translator, I have come to look at Wilbur's words with a more judicious eye, come to see his strategies and weaknesses as well as his fluidities and strengths. But my purpose here is not judgment, it's a different kind of reading. Recently, in a possibly useless attempt to understand the underwear of my own literary outfit, I decided to take a look at *Phèdre*, *Phaedra*, and *Phaedra*.

> Le dessein en est pris, je pars, cher Théramène,
> Et quitte le séjour de l'aimable Trézène.
> Dans le doute mortel dont je suis agité,
> Je commence à rougir de mon oisiveté.

> No, dear Theramenes, I've too long delayed
> In pleasant Troezen; my decision's made.
> I'm off, in my anxiety, I commence
> To tax myself with shameful indolence. (Wilbur)

> No, no, my friend, we're off! Six months have
>     passed
> since Father heard the ocean howl and cast
> his galley on the Aegean's skull-white froth.
> Listen! The blank sea calls us – off, off, off! (Lowell)

A first surprise was how difficult it was to find Lowell's *Phaedra* on the open market. You can't, except in used editions. And a second was how well the translation holds up. The more I look at Wilbur's ricochet off my work, the more I read it as a cheap shot. I still have trouble with the level of Lowell's discourse – 'off, off, off' – and his intrusions, but they are all defensible, and in some cases employ dodges I have since used in my own translations. Just after the appearance of *Phaedra*, Lowell published *Imitations*, putting forward a different, controversial vision of translation as appropriation. 'My licenses have been many,' he wrote in the introduction to *Imitations*. 'I have dropped lines, moved lines, moved

---

3 *The Classic Theatre*, volume IV, edited by Eric Bentley, Doubleday Anchor.

stanzas, changed images and altered meter and intent.'[4] Wow! Yet very little of that has to do with clarity or darkness. And very little of that licentious appropriation appears in his English version of *Phèdre*, although there are significant veerings away from the literal, wrenching the original into Lowell's own idiom.

Racine's *Phèdre* intersects nicely with both Wilbur's and Lowell's concerns. If Wilbur came to translate this particular play for its Racinian form and cadence as well as the explosive power of passion under pressure ('irrational leaps of the self-deceiving mind... sharply emphasized by the contrasting coherence of the form'), Lowell translated it for the content of madness. He did not so much make the clear things of Racine dark, but he did make them Lowell – in M.L. Rosenthal's words, 'the naked psyche of a suffering man in a hostile world'. Sometimes it seems as though he is channelling the Roman Seneca more than the French dramatist. And perhaps it was the mad anarchy of Seneca's portrayal of Nature[5] driving character to the point of insanity that appealed to Lowell in the first place.

As far as I can tell, Lowell translated no other Racine, so Wilbur's remark in the margins of my poem must have derived only from this *Phaedra*. Like Lowell, but with more precision, Wilbur translated his French alexandrines into rhymed iambic pentameter couplets. I hesitate to call Wilbur's couplets 'heroic' because their suppleness and utility seem to sit on the other side of a seesaw from the closed stateliness of Dryden or Pope. Yet they are not colloquial, a seventeenth-century formality lurks lightly within them:

> How her words chilled me! What was in her thought?
> Will Phaedra, who is still her frenzy's prey,
> Accuse herself, and throw her life away?
> What will the King say? Gods! What love has done
> To poison all this house while he was gone![6]
>    (Act III, scene VI)

Only the first line of Wilbur's here catches the rocking regularity of Racine's twelve syllables, exemplified best in 'Veut-elle s'accuser et se perdre elle-même?'. The English is brisker – 'Accuse herself and throw her

life away' – more businesslike but less menacing in its inexorability. This makes Wilbur's translations attractive for theatrical production; they suit contemporary acting styles and accessibility to audiences in our own time.

In this same passage, Lowell's lines are certainly more supple than Wilbur's, but also more hysterical, including a gratuitous reference to the weather (if only internal and psychological) to replace Phaedra's very personal *fureur*, and an editorial gloss on the poison with 'rot' to represent *funeste*.

> What now? His anger turns my blood to ice.
> Will Phaedra, always uncertain, sacrifice
> herself? What will she tell the King? How hot
> the air's becoming here! I feel the rot
> of love seeping like poison through this house.

Racine's *funeste* – 'fateful, dire', and a staple of the *vocabulaire racinien* – is a word that Wilbur has left aside completely, replaced with the filler of 'while he was gone.' (Racine is not himself innocent of such fillers for meter and rhyme.)

Wilbur's and Lowell's reputations as poets have gone up and down since the 1960s. Lowell has perhaps been more influential, but the best of Wilbur's own poems have retained their power and beauty alongside his translations.

Wilbur has also remained an influence on me as an attentive and a generous reader of other people's work. I remember an occasion when he leaned closely over a line of mine in his Wesleyan office.

'Something is wrong with the rhythm here,' he said. He paused.

He concentrated his attention on it – noticeably not appealing to me, but wrestling with something in his own reading. He leaned closer over the text, leaned back. Silence.

I held my breath, hoping for a moment of truth, the keys to the kingdom, from that master of prosody. All will be revealed.

He leaned even closer in, silently, then raised his head again. 'But everybody has his own ear.'

4 *Imitations*, p. xii.
5 '*Vindicat omnes natura sibi, nihil immune est.*'
6 *Où tendait ce discours qui m'a glacé d'effroi?*
*Phèdre toujours en proie à sa fureur extrême,*
*Veut-elle s'accuser et se perdre elle-même?*
*Dieux! que dira le roi? Quel funeste poison*
*L'amour a répandu sur toute sa maison!*

# Jacky

## FLEUR ADCOCK

*i.m. Jacqueline Simms, 1940–2021*

Let's go back in time, Jacky,
now that the present is not much fun,
to the menagerie you proposed,
entitled The Oxford Book of Creatures.

The range would be from whale to amoeba,
we agreed: Moby Dick to Cell DNA.
The whole of literature was eligible,
although with a limit on dogs and cats,

I was to find the poems, you the prose.
I plodded through alphabetical shelves
in libraries. You consulted friends,
and turned the project into a party.

Our final editorial meeting
was like a horizontal version of
varnishing day at the Academy,
with photocopies as the exhibits;

they spread all over the floor of my study
in loops and chains and winding circuits,
overlapping, sparking connections,
wandering in and out of categories.

We crawled among them, tweaking the order,
introducing them to each other:
Darwin and Pliny and DH Lawrence,
Beatrix Potter in bed with some fleas,

Richmal Crompton's William leading
a posse of rats; one of  Drake's mariners
dining on a 'a fowl whose flesh is like
a fat goose'. (We call it a penguin.)

I'll sit with your checked rug over my knees
(who else would think of arriving for lunch
with a rug instead of flowers?) Thank you,
dear Jacky, for inviting me aboard your ark.

# Four Poems

## JUNE WENTLAND

## Madame Heger does some late night needlework

Truth can be snatched from a bin
by moonlight, then smoothed flat –
the presence of love, evidenced

by needlecraft. The limits
of its professed states
jointed with a seam. White thread

detracts nothing from vocabulary,
red stabs home the pain behind
each phrase. Sentences find their own

weight when split apart – valency
when tacked neatly into place.
Should Constantin awake, pause

by the apples in the polished bowl,
ask what keeps me from our bed so late –
how to explain the fruits of samplers

such as these? 'Keeping all as it should be,'
I will say, as I stitch her *je suis*
tightly to her *délaissé*.

## MtDNA

How they might worry about me,
these mothers, mothers, mothers,

troubled by paleness of skin
worm-pink –

colour drained by several
millennia of too little sunshine.

I step out into the bone-dry dusk,
take a walk to take it in.

They rustle inside me, these Persian women,
compacted code, flesh,

unbroken thread, proceeding quick
and elegant as fruit-fly theorems. Leaves

between light, silence between bird speech
like weather systems gathering water.

## This Year

Starts with that usual extravagance
refusing to wear a day more than once,

slipping them off past chill ankles.
Air pasty as a nun's legs,

afternoons the colour of mashed tea.
Then April, cracking open

breakfast time sunny side up,
practising the spit and sizzle

of August – the larding of hips
on split fruit, sticky as Vimto.

How should I measure its passing?
Orange polish that creeps down toe nails

from ridged cuticles,
the click of ex- lovers' birthdays

that almost glitch the whirr of things.
Scented soaps like fatted calves

whose good intentions thin
them to non-existence.

Rebirth mothballed somewhere dark
and duplicitous as sock drawers.

## Bertha Bower of Hull, Pork Butcher's Daughter

The sofa was brightly coloured
when she was newly wed
but by the time I knew it
it had lost its radiance
to time-bleached green
a roughness of fabric bones
on the back of bare knees.

Sometimes she'd sing
*Velia, oh, Velia, the Witch of the Wood*
as she had when she had wild dark
hair and a rival beau who'd said:

*Bertha, you can always come to me you know,*
*if it doesn't work out with him.*
Her insistence on never wearing green –
it being the fairies' colour
so bound to bring bad luck –
was beyond denial
in that deep and reedy room
where conversation –  lacking all sharp edge –
turned between side tables
like time itself in there
sunk in something long-established,
spindle legged.

# Small Hands

### GEORGE GODDARD

Small hands, outstretched beneath cold eaves in the rain,
water cascading from *tjiwyèz* palms, dripping
from a boy's fingers imagining waterfalls
waterfalls that send ants scurrying into spaces
beneath wet leaves where I surmised they lived.
Fascinated by what seemed then,
their going-in without and emerging with wings (the ants) with which
to fly into the light       the soft light of a rainy day
at Bishop's Gap – I have not solved the mystery yet:
did they really go in wingless to emerge
having earned their wings, to soar somewhere into
another time?         And now the rainflies
are no more a source of wonderment
but a nuisance that gets between pages
of books on bookshelves and writing-tables;
and isn't this why we slay the bees into memory only
and crush iguanas into the fossil record and dolphins
into amnesia      leaving
us on a stark hillside, arms outstretched
in the bleak air, branches flailing an unforgiving sky, wondering
not in the wonderment of virginal earth, but in the repentance
of hindsight      why we did not understand sooner –
*poutji nou té ni tèt di,* why did we fly in the face of being
and not into the light.

Even now I'm afraid      that on the north-east
coast we would bruise the ubiquitous louana through which
our First Peoples named us. And so these thoughts
this morning as I dust three fallen *fonmi à zèl*
from my writing table, and the rain falls outside
and I recall a child's small fingers
cascading waterfalls down on hapless ants.

NOTE: *tjiwyèz*, Kwéyòl for inquisitive or curious (from French '*curieux*' or '*curieuse*')
*Fonmi à zèl*, Kwéyòl for 'winged ants'; *poutji nou té ni tèt di,* Saint Lucian Kwéyòl : Why we were hard-headed or
   stubborn; louana, Iguana from the Kalinago 'Iouanaloa' Land of the Iguana, Kalinago name for Saint Lucia.

# A Walk in the Dark Woods

## RICHARD GWYN

The sixth floor of the Holiday Inn at Santiago de Chile's international airport is an ideal place in which to savour anonymity. From my room I can look down on the runway, the planes neatly docked in their aprons like Dinky toys. The hotel itself, a non-place for world travellers, offers its guests a veneer of self-conscious transience, and a restaurant where we might consume generic world cuisine in a habitat devoid of any specific cultural reference. As though both to confirm and deny this sense of displacement, the hotel lobby displays a full range of multi-coloured 'Welcome' signs in around a hundred languages. I am reminded of the words of the erstwhile British Prime Minister, Theresa May, about citizens of the world being citizens of nowhere, and wonder if I share with my compatriots in Nowhereland that sad brand of homelessness of which she warned, characterised by frustration, lack of purpose and despair.

Alone in my hotel room, I can see everything going on down below: the passengers queuing at the carpark pay-booth; others dragging their wheelie suitcases across the tarmacadam towards the straggling expanse of Brutalist concrete buildings that house the Departures Hall... and if I were to open the window – which I cannot, presumably to prevent me from hurling myself earthward in horror at my own anomie – I would no doubt be able to smell the fumes of the petroleum-laden day. Like almost everything else, modern travel is a consumerist project. The gringo in the foyer with his Swedish cargo pants and Italian hiking boots, ready to head off into the Andes in emulation of Alexander von Humboldt, who is he trying to kid? What kind of a fiction is he trying to promote?

I have come to Chile to hunt down poems for an anthology of Latin American poetry that I've been commissioned to select and translate. I have, for complex reasons, left the Chileans to last. I am glad to escape the northern winter for a few weeks, but am also a little apprehensive, as this will be the last trip I undertake before settling down to the proper work of translation, whose stuttering preamble has now been underway for four years.

I am staying at the Holiday Inn because my flight from Heathrow yesterday arrived too late for me to make a connection to Valdivia, in the south of the country, where I plan to spend the first couple of weeks of the trip with my friends Verónica and Menashe. Verónica is a Chilean poet, who lived in London during much of the Pinochet dictatorship, and later Israel, where she met Menashe, a painter and ceramicist. She is a dear friend, and has offered to help me in the selection of poets from her country, with which I have been struggling.

Valdivia is a small, bustling city: the architecture and names displayed on shop fronts and, notably, on the hoardings for upcoming elections, have a distinctly Teutonic flavour. Verónica, whose own origins are Polish and German Jewish, comes to meet me at the bus station and we drive out to her house at the edge of town, surrounded by green space and woodlands, an oasis of quiet, and a perfect place to gather my thoughts on the Chilean poetry of the past half century. It is the antipodean summer, and even this far south temperatures climb into the mid-thirties.

After three days I am so immersed in Chilean poetry that I begin to feel dizzy. I keep wondering about Roberto Bolaño's provocative remarks on the subject: 'I have a vague suspicion that Chileans see Chilean poetry as a dog, or as dogs in their various incarnations: sometimes as a savage pack of wolves, sometimes as a solitary howl heard between dreams, and sometimes – especially – as a lap dog at the groomers.' What did he mean? After all, he was a Chilean poet himself, and although he became far better known – and for good reason – as a novelist, always considered himself first and foremost a poet. He spent almost all of his life after the age of fifteen in Mexico and Spain and, on returning to his native country to judge a short story competition, was less than complimentary about his fellow Chilean poets, entering into a recriminatory dispute with Raúl Zurita, which descended into a mud-slinging contest. As I read on, I learn that the enmity between Zurita and Bolaño festered until the latter's death in 2003, and even beyond, Zurita claiming as late as 2010 that he would have liked to have 'had it out' with the 'hepatic' Bolaño, an encounter which Zurita, as he himself concedes (he was by now suffering from Parkinson's disease) would probably have lost, as Bolaño was something of a brawler in his day, and his father was a boxer. I can picture the bleakly comic scene: 'In the blue corner, the poet with Parkinsons; in the red, the novelist with the knobbly liver.' The idea of this literary tussle dissolving into a grotesque fistfight between two middle-aged literary invalids is one that seems apposite within the context of Chile's poetry wars.

Since I have just been reading through Zurita's collected poetry, in search of something to translate for my anthology, I find myself returning to Bolaño's writings about Chile, among the essays, reviews and interviews in his book, *Entre parentesis,* and begin to assemble a clearer idea of his conflicted feelings about his homeland. Bolaño's casual, cavalier approach in his nonfiction writings can be distracting to the reader, just as he is distracted, constantly, in 'Fragments of a return to the native land', in which he describes the trip he took to Chile in 1998, the first visit he had made there since January 1974. He is distracted on the flight out, for example, by the very idea, or fact of flying (which he has avoided for the past twenty years) and reflects, between 'strange and vivid dreams' on the plane's engines drilling through the night, 'the night itself a plane flying inside another plane... a fish eating a fish eating another fish.'

Several pieces of writing emerged from that return trip to Chile, most notably 'The corridor with no apparent way out', in which Bolaño tells the story of a married couple's home at the time of Pinochet's dictatorship: she is a promising poet, he is a member of the Chilean secret police, and he, the husband, uses the basement of their big house in the suburbs as a torture chamber for political prisoners. In the evenings the wife holds soirées for writers, evenings of readings and wine, which sometimes turn into dinners. 'One night,' Bolaño writes, 'a guest goes looking for the bathroom and gets lost. It's his first time there and he doesn't know the house. Probably he's a bit tipsy or maybe he's already lost in the alcoholic haze of the weekend. In any case, instead of turning right he turns left and then he goes down a flight of stairs that he shouldn't have gone down and he opens a door at the end of a long hallway, long like Chile. The room is dark but even so he can make out a bound figure, in pain or possibly drugged. He knows what he's seeing. He closes the door and returns to the party. He isn't drunk anymore. He's terrified, but he doesn't say anything.'

The story reads like an allegory of some kind; perhaps, as suggested in the passage cited here, an allegory of Chile. And so it is; but it is also based in fact. The writer's name was Mariana Callejas, and she worked undercover for DINA, Chile's secret police. The husband was Michael Townley, an American businessman, who also moonlighted for the secret police. The literary workshops took place in their house in the suburb of Lo Curro, Santiago, that was procured for them by DINA. In the basement of their home, Townley interrogated leftist dissidents prior to them being shipped to detention centres where they were 'disappeared'. Rarely have literature and political violence been so graphically intertwined, but then literature and political violence was a collocation which obsessed Bolaño throughout his writing career. For him, literature was a dangerous vocation, a matter of life and death: 'Literature,' he told Luis García in 2001, 'has always been close to ignominy, to vileness, to torture.'

After spending a week working with Verónica on my translations, we – Verónica, Menashe, their daughter Tamara and I – translate ourselves to the coastal park, the *Reserva Costera Valdiviana*, where we have rented a log cabin for the weekend. The land is given over to the Mapuche people and building is prohibited within the area of the reserve. After supper that first night I take a walk under a canopy of stars, the like of which I have never witnessed, in part because I have never before travelled this far south, but also because here, the night sky, untouched by light pollution, is endowed with a unique clarity. I stand for a long while, humbled by the majesty of the heavens, the miracle of the universe, and our place within it, on our blue planet spinning its course around the sun, one among the billions of stars, only a tiny fraction of which are visible to the eye.

The region is famous for its extensive deciduous forests, and the next morning, while Menashe and Tamara go kayaking, Verónica and I visit one of them, at Los Colmillos de Chaihuín. With a guide, Alonso, we drive along an unmade forest road for an hour, having to stop several times to move logs from the track, where the mud has piled thick. When the road runs out we park up and continue on foot. The forest here contains, among other trees, canelo, alerce, and eucalyptus. The first two are indigenous, the last a moisture-hogging outsider, the villain of the piece in the local eco-system, imported from Australia and now being slowly replaced by the older indigenous varieties in a patient programme of replanting. The eucalyptus grows very quickly and self-regenerates once it has been chopped down; it can do this five times, and, given the chance, will grow to full height between each growth. South America's only marsupial, the *monito del monte* (little mountain monkey) may be found here but we are unlikely to see one as they are very shy, as is the pudú, a squat, dwarfish deer with a sweet face and dark, fearful eyes.

As we walk through this enchanted forest, I notice a bright yellow fungus, the size of a tennis ball, growing at the base of a tree, almost luminous in the dark of the woods. It is known, Alonso tells us, as *caca de duende*. There is some difficulty in rendering 'duende' into English: it can mean 'spirit', or 'creative force' as well as referring to a sprite, fairy or elf. Elf-shit sounds the most evocative translation, and the idea sticks.

We stop to pay homage to an individual tree: this particular alerce (*Fitzroya cupressoides*, a member of the cypress family) is forty-five metres tall and about 3,500 years old, according to Alonso. Its age is calculated by the girth, which is three and half metres in diameter. I reflect in astonishment that the Minoan civilisation was still flourishing on Crete when this tree was young. The forests hereabouts were once filled with alerces, but their wood was good for building boats and houses, and there are now few remaining. Although protected by law since 1976, they grow so slowly that it will be a long time before they ever repopulate the forests of Valdivia.

When the Spanish arrived in the land that would one day be called Chile, they began to exploit the rich supply of timber, useful in servicing the navy upon which the maintenance of their empire, and the delivery of its looted gold and silver, depended. It goes without saying that the destructive approach taken towards the indigenous population was extended towards the land they lived on. The earth was held as sacred by native American peoples, and the degrading of the land for material gain was utterly beyond their comprehension. But the colonial attitude towards exploitation of the natural habitat did not finish with the end of colonial rule. The governments of the new republics of Latin America – almost all of them dictatorships – continued in much the same vein as their colonial antecedents.

A dictatorship takes the tenets of colonialism and applies them to its own citizens: just as, under colonialism, the subjected peoples exist in order to serve the interests of the mother country, under a dictatorship the masses sustain the interests of the privileged few. Thus the exploitation of indigenous lands for profit (mining, logging etc), once pursued by a foreign colonial power, is carried out, under the dictatorship, by one's own rulers, as well as to whomever the country's leaders have sold off its assets, nowadays, typically, the USA or China, although historically Great Britain and France were among the principal beneficiaries.

In Chile, the Pinochet regime made sure that power was retained by the few: education was a resource to withhold in order to exercise greater control. The rail system was abandoned, in order to gain the support of road transport haulage companies and their drivers, who formed a phalanx of support for the dictator, in spite of the fact that Chile imports all its fossil fuels. An efficient rail system, it might be argued, in a long thin country, whose economic infrastructure is to a large extent determined by the shape of the land, would seem an obvious solution. However, the rail system in Chile remains unused, thirty years after the dictatorship ended. Never before had I so clearly perceived how a breakdown of responsible government affected the ecology of a country, especially in the way that logging, in this part of Chile, causes deforestation and the laying waste of the ecosystem: entire forests, that took thousands of years to grow, can be dismantled and destroyed in a matter of weeks.

Alexander von Humboldt is only now being given credit for having been the first to comment on deforestation as a destructive force, witnessing for himself, on his journeys around South America between 1799 and 1803, how the desecration of forests could not only despoil the wilderness, but wreak havoc in the ecosystem. At Lake Valencia, in present day Venezuela, Humboldt observed that extensive tree-felling was having a devastating effect on the local ecology. Trees, soil and climate were all connected, and the damage being done to the environment might, in the long run, he predicted, cause climatic changes that would be impossible to reverse. According to his biographer, Andrea Wulf, 'Humboldt was the first to explain the forest's ability to enrich the atmosphere with moisture and its cooling effect, as well as its importance for water retention and protection against soil erosion.' Two centuries on, Humboldt's ideas are finally being taken seriously, but it may be too late.

On our return from the Coastal Reserve, on the ferry across the Rio Valdivia between Corral and Niebla, I witnessed the effects of this sylvan slaughter, as the largest container vessel I have ever seen was escorted downriver by three tugs. I asked a ferry worker standing nearby where they were headed. The vessels are unloaded, he told me, onto Chinese cargo ships sitting offshore, their hulls filled to the gunwales with these chips, the material output of Chile's depleted forests.

I'm not sure how the topic arose, but driving back to Valdivia, Menashe begins to tell me the strange and terrifying tale of Paul Schäfer, who, from the 1960s, directed the 'Colonia Dignidad', near the town of Parral, which became a centre for the training and indoctrination of children into his very personal theology. The story is well known in Chile, but less so elsewhere. Born in Troisdorf, near Cologne, in 1921, Schäfer joined the Hitler Youth as a boy and served in the Wehrmacht medical corps during the Second World War. Following the war, he founded an orphanage and began preaching an apocalyptic vision of Christianity, influenced by the American William M. Branham, one of the first practitioners of televangelism, and an advocate of charismatic healing. By 1959, Schäfer was already under investigation by the German police on charges of child abuse, and he disappeared for two years, surfacing, like so many ex-Nazis (though the ex- in this case would seem redundant), in Chile.

Arriving at Colonia Dignidad, which had been settled by Germans in the 1950s as a kind of sanctuary where traditional German values and language were preserved against intrusion from the outside world, Schäfer soon re-shaped the place to fit in with his own designs, supported by others who had followed him from the Fatherland. Once in control, he encouraged members of the colony to adopt Chilean children from local communities, and established himself as an improbable Messiah, with his long grey hair and glass eye (sustained, improbably, after an accident with a dining fork). He prohibited marriage among new members, although he allowed those who were already married to remain so. All the colonists slept in dormitories and were permitted few personal possessions. Babies born in the colony were taken from their mothers and raised by 'aunts', appointed by Schäfer. Colonists worked hard, in the dairy, mills or gravel factory, in the fields and in the hospital, where care was also extended to nearby villagers: indeed, local people were especially encouraged in this regard, and mothers were sometimes told that their children had died, when in fact they had simply been abducted, to be raised in the colony. The place even boasted a hydroelectric power station. When Pinochet came to power in September 1973, the colony received a new and lucrative form of sponsorship, as Schäfer forged a close relationship with senior figures in the dictatorship, and political prisoners were sent to the colony to be tortured by agents of the Chilean secret police. According to a report by Chile's National Commission for Truth and Reconciliation, around three hundred prisoners were interrogated and tortured at Colonia Dignidad, and at least one hundred were murdered there. Poison gases were developed in the colony's laboratories, for use by the military. None of this could have been done without Schäfer's connivance and support.

Even after the return to democracy in Chile, Schäfer continued to run the colony as a personal fiefdom. His abuse of children remained unchecked, and he used a compliant physician, Hartmut Hopp, to prescribe sedatives for children in his care at the colony's boarding school, children that Schäfer drugged and raped. He continued to assault local Chilean boys until, in 1997, he disappeared, fleeing accusations of child sex abuse filed against him by the Chilean authorities. He was eventually tracked down, in 2005, to a villa in the outskirts of Buenos Aires, and extradited to face trial in Santiago.

In May 2019, the German state acknowledged the claims of many of his victims for compensation (which the Chilean government had been reluctant to award, so prolific were Schäfer's crimes). Many of these claimants had been held against their will and kept as sex slaves at Colonia Dignidad.

The Colony, renamed Villa Baviera in 1991, still exists, run by Schäfer's remaining acolytes: the colonists now draw their income from a poultry farm, which produces 30,000 eggs a day, and from tourism. The resort's Tripadvisor entry reads, in slightly off-key English: 'Cozy atmosphere for you to enjoy rest and silence in the midst of a surprising nature and first class attention.' Facilities include a man-made lake with pedal boats, a small museum (which makes no mention of the disappeared)

and a restaurant where visitors can enjoy treats such as venison, sauerkraut and smoked sausage: there is even a display of traditional dancing in lederhosen. All of this, even as the search for mass graves at the site goes on.

Relatives of the disappeared have demanded that Villa Baviera be closed, and the place honoured by a memorial to their dead. Margarita Romero, president of the Chilean Association of Memory and Human Rights, is quoted as saying: 'It is not possible that a place where serious violations of human rights such as torture, murders and disappearances take place should function as a tourist destination. Imagine a hotel built in a concentration camp in Europe – it would never be permitted.'

I cannot help but link this singular abuse of the human environment – a cult led by a Nazi paedophile in the woodlands of the lower Andes – with the despoiling of the geography in which it takes place. If we accept the term 'climate', as referring to the relations between human beings and the material conditions of their lives, then the desecration of the land and the abuse of its inhabitants – human, animal and arboreal – merge into a single sustained affront, and its reverberations touch us all.

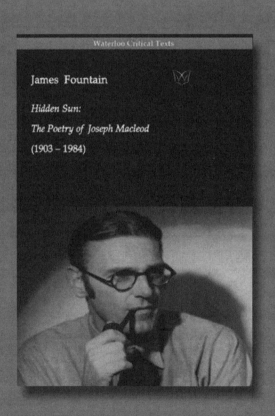

# Reviews

## The Intolerable Wrestle

Paul Muldoon, *Howdie-Skelp* (Faber) £14.99
Reviewed by Hugh Foley

Paul Muldoon's fourteenth full collection of poems, *Howdie-Skelp*, is preoccupied with junk. From the opener, 'Wagtail', where PVC roofs 'scintillate no less persuasively' than Lough Erne, to the final crown of sonnets, 'Plaguey Hill', which begins and ends with the poet's recycling bins, man-made rubbish is strewn everywhere. Though he's always been able to make magic out of insignificance, to make anything seem meaningfully connected to anything else through some nigh-impossible rhyme, there are signs in this collection that there might be too much detritus lying around now for even Muldoon to make sense of.

This worry is most fully articulated in 'The Pangolin, or Vasty'. Here Muldoon toggles between the story of bees found in a woman's eye, a gang's attempt to smuggle 'fourteen metric tons of pangolin scales' and the 'nine hundred thousand pieces of wreckage now in orbit'. The different scales, and the typically Muldonian pun on scale, create a compound image of spinning junk; the poet's efforts to make things cohere meet their match in the trash circling the earth. It's a beautiful and complex poem, puncturing the pretences of the poet as activist:

> The idea that artistic froideur is the norm
> is one that simply won't wash
> so we'll be there when the battalions form,
> standing against the King
> in his pangolin-scale armor even as we make the
> welkin ring.

The bathos here is glorious; the classic Muldoon way of letting clichés collapse under the weight of extra meaning works especially well. To make the welkin ring is to make enough noise to shake the sky, and so, seen one way, protest simply adds to the heap of trash ringing the earth.

'The Pangolin', however, is unrepresentative of the book as a whole in that it is a very good poem. While there are several fine poems, such as 'Wagtail' or 'The Bannisters', 'The Bull' or 'The Jongleurs', most of the book lacks the centripetal force holding 'The Pangolin' together. Instead, we are treated to extended noodlings on one particular kind of junk: the news.

One performance in this vein is 'American Standard', a reworking of *The Waste Land* in Muldonian tics addressed to the Trump era. Joined by Ezra Pound and T.S. Eliot, along with a Latino waiter, Virgilio, the poem's speaker tours some of the grotesqueries of recent US politics and culture, especially the violence of its border. We find risqué jokes about fratboy (or Supreme-Court-Judge-like) behaviour by Eliot and Pound, including the speaker being digitally penetrated by Eliot (a pun on doubting Thomas that may be meant to speak to the way doubt is weaponized against victims). Mostly, however, the reader has to drag their eyes over lines like these: 'Since it has rarely to do with righting a wrong or correcting an imbalance / the urge to gerrymander is rarely the urge of an honest broker.'

Perhaps, as the scholarly industry around Muldoon labours to do, you could find some brilliant etymological pun here; I found the lines themselves too dispiriting to bother. Elsewhere we get bad country songs:

> Although his uncle may have dealt in arms
> that sure don't mean a body's safe from harm.
> The killers of Khashoggi musta had nerves of steel
> when they stopped him from showing a clean pair of
> heels.

To me, such lines suggest that Muldoon thinks that the best way to make poems out of the trash choking public life and the planet is to transgress against the idea of good taste. You can find similar transgressions throughout the book, especially in the interesting failure '23 Banned Poems'.

It's not inherently a bad strategy. Questions of taste,

in art or literature are often self-aggrandizingly discussed as politics or morality in ways that really mean nothing. The carbon footprint of any book of necessary, urgent, poetic responses to the current crisis is likely to far outweigh its positive impact. 'The Pangolin' crackles with this irony. What can a poem do, atop a mountain of junk?

That poem, however, succeeds not because of its transgression, but its compression. Muldoon's attempts to work with garbage tend neither to make it beautifully compact nor retain its original pungency. A howdie-skelp, as the jacket copy tells us, is Ulster Scots for a slap given to a newborn to help it breathe, but the poems here rarely hit hard enough. Lines like 'I once met a most likely lass / who liked it mostly in the ass', from '23 Banned Poems', fall flat. They wink at us, too prissily patterned to offend, like low-fat Frederick Seidel.

When you close the book on Muldoon dutifully taking out the recycling in the tedious lockdown sonnets of 'Plaguey Hill', any demonic energy which might wake us from the stupor of the news cycle has long since dissipated. Muldoon still knows how to twist a cliché like no other poet, but too often this book is news that stays news.

## Trying again

Vona Groarke, *Link: Poet and World* (Gallery Press) £12.50
Reviewed by Kathryn Maris

In a moment of ontological despair, while walking along cliffs near Duino Castle, Rilke heard a voice say, 'Who, if I cried out, would hear me among the angels' hierarchies?' I have heard my own version of that voice while writing a poem, minus the religious fervor. It's the voice that asks, 'Who will 'hear' this poem?' or even, 'Who will care?' (The 'who' is a figure of speech, as in 'probably five people will read this poem'; but it's also a literal 'who', as in 'who *specifically* will pass judgment?'). It is the voice of lyric doubt.

If I've placed a banana peel under Rilke's impassioned lines to make a crude point, it's because I want to make a second crude point. When I upend the hyper-lyricism of Rilke's earnest and spiritual cry for help, I also upend the so-called sincerity of Rilke's poem.

These two ideas – lyric doubt and sincerity – are central to Vona Groarke's eighth poetry collection. *Link: Poet and World* examines the relationship between the lyric I and the Other, using a celestial body called 'World' (in contrast to Rilke's unspeaking angels) as mediator.

World lodges himself in the poet's house during the lockdown. He is paternal, mischievous and old-school – a cross between a tough Film Noir protagonist (he addresses the poet with the affectionate pet name 'Irish') and a toff who dons a claret-coloured smoking jacket and perfectly pleated trousers. He has a touch of the gangster too: his garish ring has a red stone that draws blood. That World comes across as a fantasy composite of twentieth-century stock male screen characters is not a weakness; on the contrary, World is cleverly emblematic of the socially distanced hours and days that many filled at home with television and film.

*Link* comprises twenty-six perfectly formed lyric poems – some classically structured, others loose or even experimental – that are answered by World in accompanying prose. Although World is not the narrator of the prose pieces, World likes to talk, engaging the poet in comedy-sketch banter.

'You think there was ever a moment, Irish, when you and I were closer? Or could be?'
'Like that first month in the womb before the Y chromosome kicks in, when all embryos are female?'

That the poet sees gender as a barrier between the female poet and the world seems fair for a woman poet of Groarke's generation in Ireland. But this is not a book of complaint: far from it. It's a book that is greedy for connection, even if adversity and antagonism are its means.

An important part of World's role is to offer the poet frequent reality checks. A tight if mysterious lyric called 'You' – which addresses an unseen, unnamed 'you' – gets this response from World: '"You and your You," says World. 'Your indeterminate but always obligingly faithful You, YOU YOU YOU YOU YOU YOU YOU YOU YOU ..."' It's an aggressive answer from World. But the aggression belongs to the poet, too. The poet continually punctures her own sincerity. She sets up an earnest lyric in order to question the clichés therein. She does this even in the lyrics themselves, such as the one titled 'Vona Groarke is writing a poem', in which she reports 'it's not going well' and adds:

How many ways can rain be turned
to something more than rain,
or the thin sticks of the alphabet be asked
to shore up a life lived glimpse by glimpse...

But she concludes (referring to herself in the third person), 'Knowing her, she'll try again. // What else would she do?' This autofictive device is self-effacing, a sending up of the poet's naval-gazing ways.

The poet badly wants to believe in poems. Even during a pandemic. Even if there is nothing new to say and no new ways to say anything. Even if – to go back to my inner voice of 'lyric doubt' – only five people read the poem. It's the kind of belief that's contagious.

And what of the link between the word and the world? The letter 'l'? 'L' is for 'lyric'. But also: a lowercase letter 'l' resembles an uppercase 'I'. So perhaps the lyric I always has been – and continues to be – a crucial link between self and world.

*Link: Poet and World* is a beautiful and innovative collection: part lyric magic, part conceptual project and part comic relief. Conceived in isolation, and fashioned by uncertainty, *Link* is a unique, poignant and witty book. Having exhausted its interaction with a private projection of World, may it now connect – as it deserves to – with the public side of the world.

## Writing with the Seams Exposed

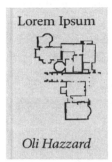

Oli Hazzard, *Lorem Ipsum* (Prototype) £12
Reviewed by Rowland Bagnall

> Digressions, incontestably, are the sunshine; – they are the life, the soul of reading; – take them out of this book, for instance, you might as well take the book along with them
> – *Laurence Sterne*

It is difficult to know how to adequately review Oli Hazzard's new book, a single, syntactically impeccable sentence of exactly 50,000 words, not least because the text itself seems not to know how to describe itself, an 'essay or zuihitsu or novel or email or monologue or text – *what is it*,' referring to a genre – 'or perhaps anti-genre' – of Japanese prose writing most famous for its loosenesses. Vaguely epistolary, *Lorem Ipsum* – whose title alludes to a randomly-generated placeholder text used commonly in typesetting – makes space for anything and everything, like Mary Poppins's handbag. In a way, I can do no better than to cite Hazzard's own review of Simone Kearney's recent collection, *Days* (2021), which seems to introduce the contours of his own book just as well: 'It registers things as they happen, anticipates events and remembers them, gets distracted by stuff in the room and by the act of composition, and describes this practice of inattention with the intimate, semi-serious, overheard frustration of the diarist.'

*Lorem Ipsum*'s cover shows the blueprint of a Cluedo-style house, hinting at the novel's own expansive architecture. Whether deliberately or not, it is reminiscent of Llanada Villa in California, Sarah Winchester's eccentric, maze-like mansion, added to throughout her life in the hope that she might somehow appease the malevolent spirits of those killed by her husband's famous lever-action rifle. While Hazzard's novel stands firm without any trickery – no false staircases or inaccessible rooms, as in Llanada Villa – the effect of reading *Lorem Ipsum* is akin to wandering the spaces of an unfamiliar building, curious to find out the particulars behind each door, discovering passageways that lead you back, quite unexpectedly, to rooms you've already explored.

In this way, the novel shares the same *in medias res* quality John Ashbery identifies in the poetry of John Clare, the poet 'already there, talking to you before you've arrived on the scene, telling you about himself, about the things that are closest and dearest to him'. It is a quality – encouraged by the gently permissive and digressive nature of the novel (following 'the Mexican- / waves of [the poet's] mind,' to borrow a phrase from *Between Two Windows* (2012), Hazzard's first collection) – that gestures to the infinite, as if the sentence might happily go on forever, never reaching a conclusion. I'm reminded of an anecdote of Mary Ruefle's, recalling Ashbery reading from 1972's *Three Poems* (fifty this year), a book that doesn't seem too far from Hazzard's. '[H]e said it was a lot like watching TV,' remembers Ruefle, as though 'you could open the book anywhere and begin reading, and flip around the book as much as you wanted to.'

Nevertheless, *Lorem Ipsum*'s format as a single, 50,000 word sentence – Hazzard alludes to Vanessa Place's *Dies: A Sentence* (2005) ('which I haven't read and probably won't read, since the idea of reading a fifty-thousand-word sentence written by someone else seems pretty gruelling') and Bohumil Hrabal's *Dancing Lessons for the Advanced in Age* (1964) as potential referents – suggests an operating system that remains profoundly linear, exploring the parameters of meaning-making within an environment (the text, but also life itself) almost comically prone to digression and distraction. One thinks of Raymond Roussel's 'La Source', with its painstaking, fifty-page description of a spa depicted on a bottle of mineral water, though the digressions of Hazzard's novel are kept neatly in check, never straying too far from the carriageway. With its frequent deviations into the particulars of parenthood (from Peppa Pig to Duplo, triggered literally, at times, by the interruption of Hazzard's children), *Lorem Ipsum* also shares something with the temporal experiments of Bernadette Mayer, as in 1982's *Midwinter Day*, composed in its entirety (so the story goes) on 22 December 1978 at the poet's home in Massachusetts: 'the present writer / At the present time'.

The temporal shiftiness of Hazzard's novel – it's difficult to decide whether his sentence might be speeding up or slowing down (perhaps it's both, or neither) – follows the suite of five procedural poems that comprise his second collection, *Blotter* (2018), in which the formal strategies at work explore a range of timeframes and their measurements. *PROGRESS: REAL AND IMAGINED* (2020), a recent book-length poem from Spam Press (in which a slice of *Lorem Ipsum* appears) is intermittently punctuated by Internet IP addresses, spatio-temporal coordinates of the poem as its being written. With *Lorem Ipsum*, Hazzard succeeds in generating an environment composed entirely of the present tense, guided by 'a gentle, pulsing, roaming form of inattention,' a Pillow Book in live-feed, a 'continuous or prolonged present' in which 'each moment [is] always happening, [...] only fully inhabited or registered by the process of trying to account for it'. Perhaps this explains the impact of the limited-edition A1 poster of the novel, printed as a lorem ipsum block against a *Clockwork-Orange*-orange background, the whole sentence apparent in a single, comprehensive glance.

What all this amounts to, more than anything, is a question about selfhood, particularly how selfhood crashes into our ideas about community and collective experience, from family, friendships and national identity to political protests, acts of terror and the experiences we share of nature, artworks, memory, and time, even experience itself, 'the lorem ipsum of our days', writes Hazzard, citing Clarice Lispector, 'the present making an incessant series of demands on our attention, *like a gate that has never stopped opening*'. Hazzard's is a novel that widens and widens, thoughtful and generous, filling and full, reflecting, with a shrug, a view of ourselves.

## Strangling the Muse

Rosanna Bruno, *Euripides: The Trojan Women: A comic*, text by Anne Carson (Bloodaxe) £10.99
Reviewed by Hilary White

Rosanna Bruno and Anne Carson's collaboration on *The Trojan Women* reimagines Euripides' classical tragedy from 415 B.C. in comic book format. Produced during the Peloponnesian War, the original play has been read as an anti-war commentary. Like the original, Bruno and Carson's comic opens with the gods Poseidon and Athene discussing how to punish the Greeks for their disrespect. In Carson's translation, however, Poseidon is not humanised but appears as a 'large volume of water'. Stranger still, Athene is 'a big pair of overalls, carrying an owl mask'. Troy is represented as a ransacked hotel. Hekabe is a sled dog, Helen alternately a fox and a hand-mirror (she changes forms), Andromache a poplar tree, and Menelaos, most remarkably, is 'some sort of gearbox, clutch or coupling mechanism, once sleek, not this year's model'.

Carson's translation, to which Bruno provided images, is as out there as this brief outline of the character-forms suggests. We are given the sense that not only has the language been translated, the form and genre transposed from one visual format to another, theatre to comic book – but that, additionally, the represented figures have been scrambled or randomised. Primarily what this does is make the reading experience a slightly surreal one, but it also on some level adds to the pathos of the story, which follows Hekabe, Kassandra and Andromache in the aftermath of the Trojan war, in which all the men of Troy have been killed, including each of

their loved ones. In a stark but also dream-like logic of representation, the characters feel once (or more) removed from their recognisable forms, and not necessarily in a way that encourages interpretation. Under the aegis of grief, where nothing makes sense, strange apparitions emerge to tell their stories. A chorus of dogs and cows, the soon-to-be enslaved population of Troy, laments the war and its aftermath. The only character to remain human is Kassandra, who is frequently referred to as 'crazy' (Kassandra, as we know from other stories, was granted the gift of prophecy by Apollo, then cursed to forever be disbelieved when she refused his advances). Here, too, she occupies a different plane to her zoomorphic counterparts. She appears carrying fire, plotting to kill Agamemnon, the man to whom she has been consigned as a spoil of war.

Bruno is known for her debut, *The Slanted Life of Emily Dickinson* (Andrews McMeel, 2017), a comic-book attempt to fill in some of the significant unknowns about the life of the poet. Bruno's artwork for *The Trojan Women* is idiosyncratic, sketchy yet evocative – fully in support of the pathos of the text, though not without moments of stark visual humour, arising largely from the surprise of seeing these strange verbal images made manifest. The animal chorus appears in mug shots, obliquely staring out from their individual panels, coming together to form the voice of the city. Hekabe, the 'ancient emaciated sled dog of filth and wrath' enters as a fully formed image, soon fading to a ghostly outline as she flounders for meaning, discounting words, discounting cries – concluding, 'can we strangle the muse?' Helen, responsible for the war in Hekabe's eyes, appears through the words of others: enframed, sometimes enlarged, a fox posing contrapuntally in stilettos, glancing provocatively over her shoulder. The possibilities of monochrome are exploited, and much is made of the opaque black background: in Andromache's most grief-stricken moment the colour scheme is inverted; she becomes a negative, her whole environment overturned.

There are occasional nods to state power through the depiction of the gods: they punish the Greeks 'because we *can*', reminisce about what 'made Troy great', and Hekabe sees 'gods at work' in the brutal levelling of Troy. Like the intertextual allusions more generally (passing references to James Baldwin via Frederick Seidel, Robert Graves, the final lines of Beckett's *The Unnameable*), these recycled phrases mainly make the comic's framework unstable, pulling in material from all worlds, haphazardly rather than systematically. The text is concerned primarily with depicting the devastation of war and the effects on those left behind, rather than making any kind of allegorical connections. Elsewhere in Carson's reworkings of the classics, the parallels drawn are more explicit; in *Norma Jean Baker of Troy* (New Directions, 2019), the stories of Helen of Troy and Marilyn Monroe are resonantly aligned. Carson has previously collaborated with the illustrator Bianca Stone on another classical reimagining, *Antigonick* (Bloodaxe, 2012), which also makes haunting use of hand-drawn imagery, to quite different effect. Bruno and Carson's collaboration is less of an artist's book than this earlier offering: *The Trojan Women* is in A4 softcover format, with black and white illustrated panels, text and image very much integrated.

It's an odd and memorable retelling whose surface wackiness belies the thoughtfulness of its multivalent translation and visual storytelling, a truly original reworking of Euripides' tragedy – one for fans of comic books and classics, and especially collaborative encounters between the two.

## Something like a conclusion in language

Michael Heller, *Within the Inscribed* (Shearsman) £14.95
Reviewed by Ian Brinton

Xavier Kalck's Foreword to Michael Heller's new collection of prose is a model of clarity. He points out to us that these essays revolve around a search for the 'sacred', and that term is to be found at the core of the whole collection: 'Heller is interested in the sacred as a sense of striving for that renewed intelligibility, which does not belong to any single doctrine, which is why he always evokes the idea of the sacred through a complex prism of perspectives, some complementary, some at odds with one another.' In addition, Kalck refers to Heller's 'dialectics of concealment and revelation', suggesting that the fullness of language invariably reminds us of the void it conceals, a notion close to the heart of Samuel Beckett whose famous words to Georges Duthuit had concerned the literary artist's 'obligation to express' as an urgency of need.

Throughout this book Heller's preoccupation with language reveals the poet's struggle 'to produce an articulation of that which was previously inarticulate'. The poet's hope is for momentary revelations, those rents in the surface of the world through which one might glimpse the infinite, and it is woven into an ongoing discussion concerning the reflective nature of the sacred. In conversation with his friend, the poet Norman Finkelstein, Heller debates the void which is left if what we see is not illuminated by any ray of meaning or direction, and it is Finkelstein who replies by pointing out that it is poetry which 'rescues history from mere facticity'.

In 'Dantean Reznikoff', a review of the Black Sparrow Press *Poems of Charles Reznikoff 1918–1975*, Heller refers to the poet's impulse to share the particularity of perception. He quotes from a letter written by Reznikoff to his wife Marie in which the New York poet had referred to his awareness of the moment, 'that slight feeling of the eye's wandering here, then there, until it forces something like a conclusion in language', a poem. Hell-

er alerts us to the haiku spirit in Reznikoff's verse, 'a complex brevity, lying somewhere between the eye's register and the semi-breathlessness of the walker who has something to tell us' and refers to two lines from a 1920 poem: ' The house-wreckers have left the door and a staircase, / now leading to the empty room of night.' As Heller perceives the power of the particular in Reznikoff's lines he recognises that here there is

No crowded metro, no petals on a wet, black bough, but rather out of a surround of lath and plaster, an ingathering of breath and then a rendering in accord with the deep loneliness of the observer who sees where the inhabitants once were and ramifies the vacancies to an almost cosmic level.

It was Osip Mandelstam in his 'Conversation about Dante' who referred to both the *Inferno* and the *Purgatorio* as glorifying the 'human gait, the measure and the rhythm of walking, the footstep and its form'. It is Michael Heller who now suggests that 'The work of literature, then, in the present is to return or, better, to strive forward toward a certain clarity, to transmute figural power into something like rhetoric, to take up the rhythms of the body and mind as argument before delight.' Given this it is no surprise to read his comments about urban living in which he loves the 'layered thickness of history, of culture'.

In an interview between Heller and Fiona McMahon 'the relationship between intellectual inquiry and lyricism' is aired and in a later discussion with Andy Fitch Heller asserts the importance of a statement by another New York poet: 'To repeat Zukofsky's "inexpressible trust in expression" is about as far as I need to go for a "poetics".'

## Exact and Abstract

Timothy Donnelly, *The Problem of the Many* (Picador) £10.99
Reviewed by Ian Pople

Timothy Donnelly's first major book, *The Cloud Corporation* was greeted with real acclaim; feted by John Ashbery, no less, as 'the poetry of the future, here, today'. So, *The Problem of the Many* has a lot to live up to. And the blurb of this edition pushes that 'lot' even further. It draws the reader's attention to the title of the book which relates to 'the famous philosophical quandary as to what defines the larger aggregate – a cloud, a crowd – which Donnelly extends to address the subject of individual boundary, identity and belonging'. No lack of ambition there, then.

The build of the poems lacks no ambition either. As in *The Cloud Corporation*, the poems usually run in long lines and long sentences across the page. So, even though the architecture of lines and line breaks often seems very carefully orchestrated, Donnelly's voice is, by and large, expansive and loping. There are shorter poems in both books, and shorter poems with shorter lines, but that voice is carefully maintained no matter the 'form' of the poem itself. That form also has a trajectory that line lengthsa and stanza lengths hold with tension and intensity.

If the title of the collection sounds a note of ambition, then the poems inside the covers do not relax that ambition. The first poem is called 'What Is Real', and other poems announce an equal reach: 'The Earth Itself', 'The Death of Print Culture', 'Leviathan', and the final poem in the book, 'Hymn to Life'. That first poem, 'What Is Real' begins:

> And though we had fed long and well at the table
> the talk always turned to whether to go on
> regardless of what it might say about our moral sense,
> regardless of what it might cost us in the end,
> or whether the time had come to surrender,

As this extract illustrates, I hope, there is a neat physical contextualizing that is easily visualized, and then the poem rolls out into much more abstract realms. Then there is that collusive 'we'. Thus, the poet is not alone and neither is the poem; both are part of a much larger dialogue with greater moral and ethical purposes. 'What Is Real' also pushes the reader into a greater sense of a teleology, a teleology of humankind. As Donnelly goes on to write, there is the hope that the particles of a life might 'recombine / into something of value, or of beauty, but humbler / than the human – not that we'd ever be able / to judge'. Thus humans might reach out to the larger notions of 'value' and 'beauty', but may well have to settle for something less. On the one hand, we might see such rhetorical reach as an honest attempt to set out the reach of the book as a whole. This is Donnelly saying, 'this is what I'm impelled to write about; here I stand I can do no other.' On the other hand, the reader is confronted with a level of pretention. It's entirely fortunate, therefore, that, for the most part, Donnelly carries it off.

Donnelly is a much more multifarious writer than this. For one thing, the cultural reference in this book is huge. From the carbonated drink Mountain Dew and its inventors Barney and Ally Hartman in Tennessee, to a walk through of Greek mythology and Callimachus, in the poem 'After Callimachus'. 'After Callimachus' itself takes in everything from the Dairy Queen fastfood's own brand of hamburger, the 'Beltbuster', to Nietzsche's view of Socrates aesthetics, and the genetic 'tinkering' with goat's milk to provide silk for military jumpsuits. And Donnelly is a wily storyteller able to weave these seemingly disparate elements into entrancing wholes.

One other important aspect of Donnelly's writing is its humanity. Although there is huge reach in these poems, and this is a volume of 198 pages, the detailing described above is not confined to Donnelly's cultural bricolage. The poem 'Wasted' starts with a description of exactly that condition:

> One thing I look forward to in an afterlife is
> a detailed spreadsheet of all the dollars I've let drop
>
> without notice to the doorstep in disarray as I yank
> my house keys out of my pocket in the dark
>
> at workweek's end, bent as I become on nothing
> more than doubling down on the bed once I make it
>
> through the door, too numb in the head to know
>   anymore
> much of what's happening down where my feet are

There is an exactness to this which is careful, plotted and very accomplished. Here, the long sentence – which continues until the end of the poem – reflects not only that movement through the door, but also the intoxicated nature of the reflection on the movement. There is mixture of the formal and slightly prissy 'detailed spreadsheet', the mimetic monosyllable of 'yank' and that almost lyrical 'workweek's end'; the lines moving carefully to that final 'where my feet are'.

On the opposite page to 'Wasted', the poem 'Cursum Perficio' ends with an equally precise evocation of sensual anticipation: 'For a long time / my cheek imagined / how the ceiling / felt against it: / cold of an otherwise / untouched plaster, / the falling away / of ancient limitation.' The words 'Cursum Perficio', 'Here my journey ends', were written on inlaid tiles at the front door of the last home Marilyn Monroe lived in, and where she died. In the poem, Donnelly contrasts Socrates and Pliny's accounts of whether swans sing at their death; Socrates suggested that swans do sing out of joy at the world they are about to enter, and Pliny denied they sing at all. Few might know the reference to Marilyn Monroe, but that and the movement from Socrates to Pliny, to Donnelly's own version of a 'swansong', makes the poem very moving.

## Reality's Ersatz

*Some Integrity*, Padraig Regan (Carcanet) £11.99
*This Fruiting Body*, Caleb Parkin (Nine Arches) £9.99
Reviewed by Maria Sledmere

'To see this & see it clearly'. So closes 'On the Principles of Alchemy': a prose poem from Padraig Regan's first collection, *Some Integrity*. This seeing happens in plural infinitives: 'To see one's life unspool in colour', 'To see a wall of ice [...] To see it melt', 'To see your father grow until he swallows God. To see him / shrink until he is a fog'. Perception transmutates; ecological, familial and spiritual traumas dissolve into a moisturised soup of confusions. To see the body as more than it seems is lyric's production, as is also the case in Caleb Parkin's recent debut *This Fruiting Body*. Both collections offer a queer, post-internet ecopoetics that is sensuous, alchemical and strange: shifting between realms of mycelia, pixelated seas and more-than-human coexistence.

Integrity is the state of being whole and undivided, but these books teem with shifting signifiers, multisensory detail, incoherence and corporeal traces. An artist's model is 'a text / I must translate / from one language / I can only / half read' (*Some Integrity*). Rather than reduce the bodies found in our orbit to coherent others, Regan and Parkin self-reflexively show up what aspects of 'Nature' and self are lost and gained in the process of writing. For Regan, this is aligned with a logic of sketching and still life: a series of dazzling, ekphrastic poems show us the descriptive 'lacquer' which hides 'a story behind' it. Such poetry offers a paralanguage for assembling ecology's im/possible household while simultaneously realising 'Everything was something, / once': in that gap between once and something is melancholia's blur.

Images of rain, dripping, slurring and melting abound in both collections. In *This Fruiting Body*, ghosts of oil spills are evoked in 'the way bodies overflow / into other bodies / no goal but to spread to engulf'. In *Some Integrity*, the tangible object behind 'Study of a Tomato' inspires liquid negation:

It does not speak. It is not
a symbol for menstruation

or the absence thereof.
This is this & only this.

Regan asks us to consider likenesses (blood/tomato juice) as sites of both trouble and play, presence/absence and desire. A poem named after Han van Meegeren's fake Vermeer, *Supper at Emmaus*, reminds us that 'people always want what isn't there'. To be 'only this' and not 'a symbol' is to insist on a contingent materiality, juicy as Ponge's orange, yet 'soft & softer' – always undergoing the process of resolving into identity, coming to form this unstable sign. As menstruation is the cyclical reminder of fertility, its (non)appearance queers naturalised notions of embodied, literary (re)production. Also dripping between stanzas, rainfall waters the poem as it does many others to a tender recovery, an uncertain outline. The speaker queries, in measured tones, what is the ethics of writing the 'It' which cannot speak back?

There is melancholy in Regan's negation, also expressed in forms of rent and tearing which reject the possibility of integrity (as we see in the bullet-shot fruit of '*Pomegranate*', or the knife-gouged 'A Pumpkin'). Catriona Mortimer-Sandilands describes melancholia as 'a form of socially located memory in which the loss

of the beloved constitutes the self', for whom it becomes 'a form of preservation of life – a life, unlike the one offered for sale in ecotourist spectacle, is already gone, but whose ghost propels a *changed* understanding of the present'. The keen precision of Regan's poems studies a situated ecological melancholia, where 'the beloved' is something like the dying fruit of the world, weathered and punctured with the arrest of what's changed.

As Regan offers a reflexive alchemy of language itself, Parkin works by accretion: not dissimilar from the 'additive and accretive' logic that Eve Kosofsky Sedgwick identifies as the 'desire of a reparative impulse' within queer trauma. In an ecological world that is broken, haunted and saturated with grief, Parkin looks for reparative signs of life, affection and joy – from the compost bin to the glossary, and the 'flotsam afterlife' below a writing shed. Playing with form – Keatsian odes, love missives, trauma fugues and occasional poems – *This Fruiting Body* performs through sheer proliferation its titular acts of mushrooming, bloom and bearing. At times, I'm reminded of Bernadette Mayer's 2016 collection, *Works & Days*, in the deft and cheeky way Parkin inhabits a sapling epistolary:

Dear Trees,

Is it wrong we objectify you this way?
[...]
Yours suspiciously,
Saplings
('Tree Triptych')

Of course, trees produce the stuff of the paper upon which the book is printed, and any poem about trees might be a comment on the mulch of poetry's precarious environs. In this staged letter between arboreal generations, there is both a curiosity and vulnerability of poethical exchange, accompanied by the amiable wink of camp. Elsewhere in the collection, Parkin deconstructs the gender economies of the outdoor store, the everyday microaggressions of heteronormative society and the intimate life of a hermit crab, offering a generous plenitude of eco-critiques and encounters within late capitalism.

This is also a post-internet ecopoetics. Regan and Parkin explore how the most seemingly instinctive of environmental affects are in fact filtered, refracted and reproduced through virtual realms of gifs, video games and language itself. To problematise integrity through collage, erasure and lyric excess is not only to tear open the unified liberal self but also to raise the spectral, xenomorphic otherness of Nature's mediation. The fruiting body of a search engine's 'terms of service' is reimagined as a 'MyCelium' network (Parkin); the 'Glitch City' of 'invalid tile data' found in old Pokémon games offers a slippery *oikos* for supplementing loss (Regan). Like code or India ink, poetry 'performs its tiny fractal / creep' (Regan) through the messy filaments of existence; in Parkin, the Megadrive icon 'Ecco the Dolphin' thrashes in the textures of 'digital habitat':

Ecco is neat between the lines like practice

handwriting, before the dark ink overspills

the edges of its enclosure.
(Parkin, 'Ecco the Dolphin')

In this medial realm of eco-écriture, poetic form is the arbitrary edge of 'enclosure' from which the lyric subject departs as 'overspills' of force. Both collections relate the 'grinding and ordinary cruelty' (Regan) of compulsory heterosexuality to the slow violence of ecological disaster, punctuated with moments of intensified crisis and harm. In such a world, Ecco's iterative 'neat' swim is survival's bleeding edge.

If language loads us into particular modes of being, this poetry offers the brilliant and perverse necessity of 'warping' presence to what doesn't necessarily 'exist' (Regan, 'Glitch City'). In pursuit of the echo-locative, of the 'fever dreams' (Parkin) of 'emotional memory' (Regan), both collections sound out the glitches of moments 'when the system shows its freakish, unplanned depths' (Regan). When the language of fossil capital exposes the sporous commons which is its possible understory, its dark ecologies of consumption, its (im)probable fidelities and lusty residues. Attending to the material economies of poetry as placemaking, a resource of 'brackish meaning' (Parkin) in a world of enforced scarcity, where 'even our ghosts / can't fill us', these works ask:

What isn't theft
now that even the seas are watered down?
(Regan, 'History')

## Perilous laps

Selima Hill, *Men Who Feed Pigeons* (Bloodaxe) £12
Hannah Lowe, *The Kids* (Bloodaxe) £10.99
Reviewed by Carla-Rosa Manfredino

The seven sequences in Selima Hill's *Men Who Feed Pigeons* are linked by relationships, mostly between a man and a woman, narrated by a woman observing a man. The poems make deceptively simple statements, 'He is one, and I the other, gender' ('Childhood Sweetheart'), but carry deeper, darker meanings.

Each poem is like the piece of a jigsaw and seems to reflect the book's overarching question: can we ever fit comfortably with another person? This uncertainty plays throughout and can be seen in the stacking and de-stacking of images. Cake features in many of the poems: 'The

man whose tea is never hot enough/ is peering at the row of fancy cakes / that may look good to everybody else / but not, as a promise that is never fulfilled' ('His Victoria Sponge'), and 'a wedding cake deep inside its icing / is concentrating on not thinking *knife*' ('Wedding Cake').

There is a sense that deeper feelings are being avoided, or brushed over with something lighter. They find their way into the poems obliquely, however, as in 'Golden Sands', where the speaker says, 'We've suddenly found ourselves alone / and feeling all the feelings of the tenderness / we came out here to try to forget'. And in the description of the patient who 'slides across the ward like a door // that leans against the nurse as if to say / *please can she be sparing with the truth*' ('The Patient').

In one of the marriage poems, 'Snowdrop', the speaker says 'You love me like a man loves a bird / on whose tiny white foot he slips a tiny ring', suggesting the trickier side of marriage and nodding to the book's title. There is a sense that the humans in *Men Who Feed Pigeons* are part of an experiment and are being observed for their peculiarities. And it isn't just romantic relationships that are examined. A son is 'forty, and obese, / and on the day she suffocated him // she says she asked her son one last question: / *Can't you just be normal?* But he couldn't' ('The Son').

The layering and delayering of images and their subsequently changed meanings is particularly skilful. Hill makes unexpected turns in these poems that change the tone completely, 'everybody marvels! Chess is easy – // difficult. / Like sitting on his lap' ('The Uncle'). Throwaway statements are scrutinised, '*You either love a person or you don't.* / That's what I've been told but it's not true' and curious deductions are made, 'Celeriac is not the same as celery / a boyfriend's not the same as an ex' ('The Ex'). The beauty of these delightful, strange poems lies in their puzzlement and their refusal to explain things away. *Men Who Feed Pigeons* invites the reader to connect and reconnect its meanings, offering a unique lens through which to view our most ordinary exchanges.

Hannah Lowe's *The Kids* is a gritty collection of modernised sonnets about the poet's time as a teacher in an inner-city London sixth form, alongside poems for her younger self and her own teachers. The book is a reminder that teaching is something we encounter throughout our lives and from different people. The poems about teaching are varied and reflect on the ways in which class, race and gender intersect at school, especially in a city. Lowe illustrates the beauty of multiculturism, and the challenges both student and teacher face in the midst of it.

Violence and love are inextricable in the book. In 'Blocks' Lowe writes about her child self, 'In that house of risk – unstable, unwell – / where often I was thrown like a paper jet / downstairs' and the strength she gained, 'That name I wrote for myself, / over and over, standing up for itself'. Elsewhere, in a poem about her mother she writes, 'She brought me a glass of orange squash each morning / and hers was the strong soothing hand that led me / to school [...] *My mother?* She grabbed me by the collar too' ('She').

Now Lowe is a mother and perhaps learning the most

important lessons of all. In 'Daughter' she captures the bond between her children, 'when I tuck her in, her sugary whisper / in my ear – asks me if her brother's asleep. / Can't let herself go down, until she knows/ he's sunk below the slumber ground' and their inevitable independence from her, 'When I go to speak, she turns away, / dives down, and swiftly swims away from me'.

Lowe has lived through a time when technology has changed teaching, 'Suddenly computers, / screens, an electronic pen / so off the cuff' ('Technology') and how children spend their time, as in 'Sonnet for Boredom', where she watches her son 'and the iPad is a raft / he sails from breakfast to lunch on, lunch to dinner [...] When I was six, my game // was boredom'.

*The Kids* draws connections between people whilst underlining their separateness. In 'House' she writes, 'Where everyone I loved/ lay and dreamt their solitary dreams' and in 'Ni hao', as a mother observing her son lying in bed beside her, 'is this what aloneness is?... this small boy flowering beside me?'. Lowe reminds us that we learn from each other at every stage of life, and that some of our greatest lessons are learnt outside the classroom.

## Displaying Our Dead

Joelle Taylor, *C+nto: & Othered Poems* (The Westbourne Press) £10.99; Gail McConnell, *The Sun is Open* (Penned in the Margins) £9.99
Reviewed by Dominic Leonard

As the epigraph of Joelle Taylor's T.S. Eliot Prize-winning book points out, *cuntare* means, in Latin, 'to sing' or recount a story. The '+', if pronounced *and*, turns the title from a censored word to a *canto*, a poetic term ultimately tied to Dante's journey of self-discovery, also from the same Latin root of song. This plus, too, simultaneously reminds the reader of the multiplicity of sexual identity that open-endedly punctuates the acronym LGBTQ+. Before we reach the first page of *C+nto*, then, the directions this book will take us in are clear: a pilgrimage of sex, song, and the growth of a personal identity.

Taylor is interested in how cultures and groups change and adapt, particularly how older generations of queer pariahs find themselves interacting with newer generations who, perhaps, take their freedoms for granted: 'we display our dead our old / ways our bedroom bunkers // the presence of absence'. There are lacunae in the fabric of contemporary queer spaces, and Taylor's project is to sound the depths and plumb 'the archaeology of the dancefloor'. Lived queerness is fashioned out of rejection:

'you cut your first suit out of the thick silence when you enter a room,' this excellent metaphor summarising both how much clothing matters in a very literal sense, but also in the sense of how signifiers and cultural codes can both help and hinder the queer experience (butchness, in this particular case): 'the descent of (out)laws...they fear you.' Lesbians are 'sterile and barren     an un-useful female    empty as church pews'; the body is a 'political placard', as if the shape and size and message of the queer body is the message itself, an open rebellion: 'my gender / is exile'.

The book's central movement, titled 'C+NTO', is figured as a boxing match fought out in 'Rounds'. I am less convinced by the form in these poems – prose broken up with gaps in the lines which usually match the clause or sentence-endings – which may co-ordinate with the way the poems are performed aloud, but ultimately don't add much to the experience of reading on the page. Although Taylor's electric live performances of her poems are arguably what make the biggest impact, her handling of the line on the page is skilful and only sometimes reads as arbitrary page recordings of something which lives on-stage. Her lines are mostly short and abrupt, eschewing conventional punctuation to nod towards the existence of the text outside of its printed form whilst also carrying a narrative at skilful speed. Occasionally well-handled pentameters take on spoken-word's typically falling, dactylic rhythms: 'The jawline remembers // winding the words in; maybe the skin knows / something about silence, see how it has turned // from itself.' The lines are not merely units of syntax or sense; the enjambment is tactful, and the line breaks regularly help to carry a narrative moment to its fruition, or to engender a moment of surprise.

The section 'O, Maryville' is a Ginsbergian escapade down a main road in London, featuring a psalm to the bar of the poem's title: 'for thine are the body / the birthing & the burning / forever & ever // are you a man?' This twist is characteristic of Taylor's ability to find comedy and tragedy side-by-side: the amen is caught in the throat, and Taylor bastardises the completion of prayer and turns it into a reminder of the homophobia that exists even in queer spaces which are supposed to be sacred. There are, occasionally, lines which resort to easy wins and generalisations ('men     are broken things     breaking things'), but these are weighed out by her smarter twists on cliché: 'what does not kill you     makes you make you.' At her best, the poems in this book are moving, funny and, despite their seriousness, joyful and *fun*; a good night out is something rarely found in book-length collections.

*The Sun is Open* by Gail McConnell is an exhumation of 'public and private materials,' relating to the death of the author's father, killed by the IRA in 1984. '[W]hat does it all add up to,' the poet asks: 'not a murder book and not an archive not a fever not a feeling... it's what dislodges in my body'.

The poems' form is consistent across nearly the whole book: prose poems in rectangles amalgamate original writing and text lifted from sources as various as McConnell's father's journal, news reports, and the Bible.

These have a visual resemblance to newspaper cut-outs, archive boxes to be unpacked, and coffins. The lifted text is in grey rather than black, which has a number of visual effects: the text from a different source is like a ghost in the machine, denoting the extraneous nature of the data as well as the struggle of bringing external logic to an explosive, unexplainable event (the violent death of a loved one): an intentional ghost living in the fabric of the text. Similarly, through each page, the next poem can be seen in the exact same space on the reverse page, a grey shadow through the paper's texture. This, too, adds to the ghostly sense of loss which informs the whole book, particularly this latter ghost, which is an artefact of book production, but one which draws attention to the book's existence as a living archive. It is a smart innovation, which unites the book's form with its politics in a way that is completely unique and effective.

The form also incorporates fragments across the page, making the blank rectangles look occasionally like erasure poems. This can have formal and syntactic benefits. One fragment reads, 'copy all this out and I won't have to address you' and then, further down the blank page, 'shit'. This can be read as 'I don't have to address anything to you', or a mere expletive interpolation at the realisation of the address's impossibility – or both simultaneously. Or, another example: 'bullets sailing through the blue air into perforation into a heap of gravel an almost human shape into death into silence or whatever       comes next'. The gap, an internal enjambment like one of Berryman's, prompts multiple syntactic readings: 'whatever comes next', but simultaneously the hanging 'whatever', like an exhaustion of retelling that is partnered with the possibility of life after death, in any form. McConnell's ability to lead us in a number of directions simultaneously is one of her finest skills, and one which serves the book for multiple re-readings.

The poems are without punctuation, each section comprising one running sentence incorporating both the grey and black text into a seamless, meandering unit of meaning, but one at the edge of which danger is constantly shimmering: 'no noise outside a bird sometimes a helicopter', and even an erasure of Psalm 23 is creeping with menace: 'my enemies see me know my house'. With this fragmentation being so inherent to the poems' life, it is often hard to follow a sentence's syntax until it is read aloud, making them disorienting and obfuscated, contributing to their sense of becoming; the poems are in a state of discovery, still raw from the event that prompted them, and the text lifted raw, like ore, from its many sources. The journalistic narrative is not only engendered by its form, but the overwhelming quantity of information, the cutting and pasting, like a scrapbook made in mourning to try and piece disparate ideas and voices together (like Anne Carson's *NOX*). As the poet puts it, it is 'easier to take what I have found and break it up...glue it back the wrong way.' This kintsugi fragmentation is shored against the ruin of the absence made present, the ghost in the poet's life which fills the hollow places of the book's fragmented text. Like another Penned in the Margins release, Sarah Hesketh's *The Hard Word Box*, *The Sun is Open* is a valuable addition to the troubling question of form's political and investigative responsibilities.

## Nuts in May

John Clegg, *Pinecoast* (Hazel Press) £10
Ella Duffy, *Rootstalk* (Hazel Pres) £10
Helen Mort and Katrina Naomi, *Same But Different* (Hazel Press) £10
Reviewed by Rory Waterman

I've heard it said that chapbooks are named thus because they are – or were – 'cheap'; chap, in this old wives' etymology, is simply a bastardisation of that word. It isn't true, of course. In any case, it is generally rare that chapbooks, or pamphlets, are especially modestly priced – and these days some presses go in for objets d'art that cost as much as collections. The manifestly collectible pamphlets in the Clutag Five Poems series, for example, are equally exquisite and minimalist in design, using simple ingredients of the highest quality, like much of the finest Italian cooking.

Comparable things might be said about the saddle-stitched pamphlets from Hazel Press. This publisher focuses on environmental matters, and probably does a good job at keeping paper consumption down, because each pamphlet will set you back a tenner. The press also doesn't seem to see the point in biographical notes or blurbs, so a reader has no choice but to jump straight into the poems. They publish a lot of good things, though, and this review will focus on three of the recent highlights.

John Clegg's *Pinecoast* contains two short groupings of poems – eight pages each. The first is set in various locations around southern England and the second in Quebec. Clegg's syntax sometimes gets the better of him, which is a surprise because he's a superb prose stylist. Nonetheless, there are some evocative and otherwise finely tuned lyrics here. 'Small Array' recalls working as a mower at Mullard Radio Astronomy Observatory in Cambridgeshire:

I saw one dis
locate itself – near dawn –
it rattled twenty foot downline
and dipped its pitch a very
little, to a different star.

And unlike Edward Thomas's middle of England, 'Cambridgeshire on every side / seemed depthless'. Other poems are part-fable, alive with Clegg's idiosyncratic and enjoyable imagination: 'I helped a boneless ghost to cross a stile.' The Canadian poems are the prize, though, full of warm wonder and agile shifts between perspective. Bears

disappear into the maple stands
and out of sight are out of sound;
it's not their tact,
it's trees which close behind them.

Regarding a sea eagle ('"patience in its rest of cruelty / that waits and does not seek for prey" / says Michael Field, though not about sea eagles'), he muses that 'No strength wields itself like reserve strength. / No elegance even – she can afford to wobble on thermals.' Every poem here has something about it. That's rare.

Once in a while, a poetry collection comes along to augment what it is we think books of poems can do. Rarely, at least since the middle of the last century, are they avowedly avant garde works. Here is a recent example: Claudia Rankine's *Citizen*. I think the same, broadly, can be said about Alice Oswald's *Dart*, the first of several recent long poems or sequences about rivers, and several others in multiple voices. Ella Duffy's *Rootstalk* bears that mark, without feeling at all derivative. The poem is written in the reimagined voices of five historical or mythological figures, each indicated by a square-bracketed name in the margin, all of whom are for some reason obsessed with the ghost orchid, a rare orchid that only breaches the earth's surface to flower about once a decade. It's a bizarre conceit, but the poetry is vivid and dramatic for all that: 'In the otherworld, there are wild boar / and there are women deadheading', says Persephone. And, at the end, Demeter closes things out, the quest incomplete:

when my daughter was young and imagining spring,
she would talk to me through flowers; things she felt
she couldn't say,
arranged in a vase in the kitchen.

I arrive at the place where the missing are found and
start digging.

So this is a subtle, complex poem: a multi-voiced piece about failures to communicate, embodied in the search for a flower that hides without knowing it does so.

*Same But Different*, by Helen Mort and Katrina Naomi, is a boring title for a pamphlet of poems by two often excellent poets. It's also not very accurate, at least in one sense, because in some cases the words they have used for prompts ('Instrument', 'Gift', 'Future', etc) are the only things the corresponding poems have in common; they appear to have written one poem each to ten such prompts. However, the pamphlet contains no contextualising information, nor even authorial attributions to the poems, so my claim that they have contributed ten poems each might be wrong.

Other poets have done comparable things in recent times, of course. Last year, Anthony Caleshu and I edited *Poetry and Covid-19* (Shearsman, 2021), an anthology of nineteen collaborations between two poets, sometimes working with a translator, and a few of them follow the same apparent methodology as Mort and Naomi. And Alan Jenkins and John Kinsella quite recently published a full collection of unattributed poems, *Marine* (Enitharmon, 2016), though their individual styles are so distinctively separate that they might as well have labelled each one. The same cannot be said for Mort's and Naomi's styles, or at least the styles of these poems. Mort has a particularly distinctively image-laden approach, and tendency towards sudden small and touching epiphany, that sometimes seems to give her away. For my money, for example, 'Piano' is one of hers: 'perhaps', the poet writes, her father

trundled it through the peeling gate
the whack of its heavy spring
resounding inside mahogany

perhaps that was the way
he sounded goodbye

As is 'Wash', with its 'sky / that puts the valley / in a bowl and gently / holds it under'. This is crisp, imagistic writing, and there's a lot of it here. Most impressive, though, are the poems that unsentimentally evoke human realities:

My mum used to catch me out: which is heavier,
*a tonne of bricks or a tonne of feathers*?

She'd laugh. *There's no difference*. Now her limbs
are tricking her. Her body was a house.
Now it's made of feathers.

What is it in us that desires to put a name to such a personal anecdote? But we can't, and of course the circumstance the poem evokes – or something similar to it – is likely to come to everybody. The punctuation again goes awry in some of these pieces, such as 'Hare', which ends with a full stop and yet contains two run-on sentences. I can't believe such inconsistency is deliberate – it certainly serves no function – and an editor should spot such things even if a poet doesn't. But this is an intriguing project, and these are alert poems.

# Contributors' Notes

**Julian Brasington**, printmaker, lives in Llanfairfechan. His poems have appeared in *Stand, Ink Sweat & Tears, Envoi*, and other magazines. He is working on a series of prints which marry visual image and verse. **George Goddard** is a Saint Lucian writer. His debut collection of poems, *Interstice*, was published in Saint Lucia in 2016. **Hsien Min Toh** edits the *Quarterly Literary Review Singapore* and is the author of *Dans quel sens tombent les feuilles* (Paris, 2016). **Stav Poleg**'s debut poetry collection, *The City*, was published by Carcanet in Spring 2022. Her work has appeared in *The New Yorker* and *New Poetries VIII* (Carcanet 2021), among others. **Ian Brinton**'s most recent publications include *Language and Death*, a translation of poems by Philippe Jaccottet (Equipage, 2022) and a translation of Baudelaire's 'Tableaux Parisiens', (Two Rivers Press, 2021). **Kit Fan**'s poetry collection *As Slow As Possible* was a Poetry Book Society Recommendation and one of the Irish Times Books of the Year. His debut novel is *Diamond Hill*. **Matilda Hicklin** is a translator, writer and poet with particular interests in machine translation, post-editing and contemporary Russian poetry. She will shortly begin her PhD studies in Translation at the University of Bristol. **James Campbell**'s latest book, *Just Go Down to the Road: A memoir of trouble and travel*, was published in June. Under the name J.C., he wrote the NB column in the *TLS* for twenty-three years. A book based on the column, from which the extracts in this issue are taken, is forthcoming from Carcanet in the autumn. It will also include original essays on life and work at the *TLS*. **Hugh Foley**'s poetry has appeared in *Poetry Review, Poetry London, The Boston Review* and *The Rialto*, among other places. His critical book, *Lyric and Liberalism in the Age of American Empire*, is forthcoming this year with Oxford University Press. **Hilary White** is a writer and researcher based in Manchester, currently working on sleep disorder and experimental poetics. Her writing appears in places like *Banshee* and *The Stinging Fly*. She is one third of the poetry collective, No Matter. **Carla-Rosa Manfredino** is a freelance writer and tutor from the Conwy valley, Wales. **Dominic Leonard** was born in West Yorkshire. He won an Eric Gregory Award in 2019, and his pamphlet, *Dirt* (2021), is published with Broken Sleep. Maria Sledmere lives and teaches in Glasgow, as editor-in-chief of SPAM Press. Her most recent books include *String Feeling* (Erotoplasty Editions, 2022) and *The Luna Erratum* (Dostoyevsky Wannabe, 2021). **Rowland Bagnall**'s first collection (*A Few Interiors*) was published by Carcanet 2019. He is currently enrolled as a PhD candidate in Creative Writing at the University of Birmingham. A selection of his work can be found at www.rowlandbagnall.com. **Catherine-Esther Cowie** was born and raised on the island of St Lucia and now lives in the US. Her work has appeared in *TriQuarterly, Prairie Schooner* with work forthcoming in *RHINO Poetry*. **Tuesday Shannon** is an M4C and AHRC PhD Candidate and Associate Lecturer at Nottingham Trent University. Her poems have featured in *Wild Court*, Soundswrite Press' *Take Three: Volume 1*, and others. **Fleur Adcock**'s most recent collection is *The Mermaid's Purse* (Bloodaxe, 2021). In 2019 her *Collected Poems* appeared from Victoria University Press, Wellington, New Zealand. She lives in London.

*Editors*
Michael Schmidt
John McAuliffe

*Editorial Manager*
Andrew Latimer

*Contributing Editors*
Vahni Capildeo
Sasha Dugdale
Will Harris

*Proofreader*
Maren Meinhardt

*Designer*
Andrew Latimer

*Editorial address*
The Editors at the address on the right. Manuscripts cannot be returned unless accompanied by a stamped addressed envelope or international reply coupon.

*Trade distributors*
NBN International

*Represented by*
Compass IPS Ltd

*Copyright*
© 2022 Poetry Nation Review
All rights reserved
ISBN 978-1-80017-285-2
ISBN 0144-7076

*Subscriptions—6 issues*
INDIVIDUAL–print and digital: £45; abroad £65
INSTITUTIONS–print only: £76; abroad £90
INSTITUTIONS–digital only: from Exact Editions (https://shop.exacteditions.com/gb/pn-review) to: PN Review, Alliance House, 30 Cross Street, Manchester, M2 7AQ, UK.

*Supported by*

Supported using public funding by
ARTS COUNCIL ENGLAND